IER?

306
ART

Arterburn, Jerry
    How will I tell
my mother?

Date Due

HOW WILL I TELL MY MOTHER?

JERRY ARTERBURN
with his brother
Steve

A Division of Thomas Nelson Publishers
Nashville

Published in Nashville, Tennessee, by Oliver-Nelson Books, a division of Thomas Nelson, Inc., Publishers, and distributed in Canada by Lawson Falle, Ltd., Cambridge, Ontario.

Scripture quotations are from THE NEW KING JAMES VERSION. Copyright © 1979, 1980, 1982, Thomas Nelson, Inc., Publishers.

Scripture quotations noted NIV are taken from the HOLY BIBLE: NEW INTER-NATIONAL VERSION. Copyright © 1973, 1978, 1984 by the International Bible Society. Used by permission of Zondervan Publishers.

The Scripture quotation noted NASB is from the New American Standard Bible, © The Lockman Foundation 1960, 1962, 1963, 1968, 1971, 1972, 1973, 1975, 1977, and is used by permission.

Most names and events have been fictionalized for protection of privacy and maintenance of confidentiality.

Printed in the United States of America.

Library of Congress Cataloging-in-Publication Data

Arterburn, Jerry, 1950–
    How will I tell my mother? : a true story of one man's battle with
  homosexuality & AIDS / Jerry Arterburn, with his brother Steve.
     p. cm.
    ISBN 0-8407-9555-6 (pbk.) : $7.95
    1. Arterburn, Jerry, 1950–   . 2. Gay men—United States—
—Biography.   3. AIDS (Disease)—Patients—United States—Biography.
4. Homosexuality—Religious aspects—Christianity. I. Arterburn,
Stephen, 1953–   . II. Title.
HQ75.8.A77A78   1988
306.7′662—dc19   88–3763
                                                       CIP

3 4 5 6 — 92 91 90 89

To

my wonderful family,
whose help and understanding
have inspired me to persevere

Contents

Part Two

Foreword

One of my greatest blessings is having three sons, Terry, Jerry, and Steve. Being their mother has always presented my greatest challenges. Although I have experienced some times of deep despair, I would not change my role if I could. Through my mother role, I learned to exercise unconditional love and came into a closer and more meaningful walk with the Lord. And I learned to cope with things boys cherish: pockets full of rabbits' feet, frog skin, marbles, pieces of string, and buttons torn from shirts. Our third son was as distinct as our first and second, which means I had three unique individuals with whom to work through all their years at home. It was busy, tiring, wearing, fun, exciting, fearful, and questionable. There was little quiet time amid their various activities.

My husband, Walter, and I came from similar spiritual and economic backgrounds, but there were considerable differences. His parents were close-knit and were emotionally stable. My father's Monday through Friday absence from the home, due to work-related travel, created intense stress between my mother and father. As a result, there was criticism and negative complaints regularly. Six years after I left home and married, my father killed himself. And although I had been away from home for several years, his untimely death was a shock and a deep heartache.

In our early years in Ranger, Texas, Walter was wrapped up in the boys and their activities. He coached Little League and spent time with the boys in all their endeavors. When we moved to Bryan, he became more absorbed in his business and more active in the church. During that time Walter withdrew from much of the child-rearing responsibilities and left most of them up to me. He was and is a loving father, concerned and interested in his sons' lives; I was more the disciplinarian.

During our boys' growing-up years, Walter and I were busy making a living and trying to see that they had a good education and good Christian teaching. We were a Christian family and regularly attended church, Sunday school, prayer meeting, Training Union, and Sunday night Bible study. Walter and I had grown up this way, and we thought it was the best way to raise our boys. I always thought our family lived fairly normal and routine lives.

As the boys grew, they spent several weeks each year at Christian camp, worked at odd jobs in the summer, visited grandparents and other relatives, spent holidays with family groups, and took some vacations to various places. When they graduated from public high school, each went on to college. All three boys dated and were actively engaged with various social and academic functions. They were well liked by both boys and girls and made friends easily. After obtaining their college degrees, Terry and Steve married, and Terry had four children. Jerry still had not married by age thirty-five. But since he was deeply involved with his career and surrounded by friends, we weren't concerned. He had plenty of time, we thought.

The news that Jerry was homosexual was a total shock. I was filled with fear and disbelief. I felt betrayed, trapped, and very frightened. Many emotions were released in me—guilt, shame, anger, failure, self-pity, dread. I felt torn, fragmented, wounded, and mentally helpless. For someone without faith in a forgiving God, it might have been easier to die or lose her mind. But God is the Lord of my life and the Lord of my family, and I did not die or go insane. With His help I am surviving. Not only was I pained to discover that Jerry was homosexual, I was anguished to learn that he had the deadly virus AIDS. The impact of his vulnerability and grave condition hit me at once. What can help but a miracle? I pray every day for the medical discovery of a cure of some kind for this menacing killer of our world's precious sons and daughters. Jerry's death is certain without it.

I know what it means to be a crushed and broken mother. I also know the grace of God in this situation. Yes, there have been moments, even days, when I have known nothing but pure despair and sorrow. I have at times felt cheated, having poured all of my life into my precious boys, only to have one son threatened because of Satan's power and ability to destroy so much God-given potential. There is no simple way to face the heartbreaking humiliation of a dying son who made the choice to misuse his body. The AIDS virus has hurt Jerry both mentally and physically. But I am grateful, with all my being, to tell you that he is spiritually a whole person in Jesus Christ. Jerry has repented of his sins. He has been redeemed by the shed blood of Jesus. The cross upon which Jesus died has become Jerry's hope for eternal life, with even greater meaning than before. God has sent His Holy Spirit to guide and comfort Jerry. Not only has Jerry made his life right with God, he has asked our forgiveness and we have given it. You will learn Jerry's story as you read the book.

From a pit of hopelessness, hope rises nonetheless, rising every day, more and more. God's loving mercy is the most outstanding gift I have ever known. What have I learned from this experience that may be helpful to you? I have learned that when God gives a mother a child, He gives love for that child regardless of the circumstances of that child's life. It is God alone that makes a mother. I have learned that God delights in touching fragmented lives and making them whole. I have learned that God uses pain, shame, and disappointment to humble those whom He loves. God proves His love for me by using others to love both me and Jerry unconditionally. My sister, Mary, has been a tremendous source of encouragement in many helpful ways. She has consistently expressed love and acceptance to the two of us. At times she was the only one with whom I could share my most dreaded fears. She was always there. She brought her dear friend and Bible teacher, Betty, to share with us. She has taught us some of the ways of God that have been most helpful to our family. And she has loved and prayed for us, counseled and encouraged us. My sister has always been sensitive to needs and has always loved our boys as her own.

Walter, who suffers the same loss as I, is a wonderfully caring and sensitive husband. He has been the source of a constant flow of love into my life. I thank God for him and pray daily for the healing of his broken father's heart. God seems to use mothers to fix many things. How do you fix a broken heart, God? I believe it is God's thought that continues to come to me, *Use love and not Band-Aids.* Love is God's fix in every situation, every day, over and over again. Unconditional love is my constant response to Jerry. I feel nothing that is not loving and forgiving.

Do I have questions? Yes, many. The homosexual lifestyle and all its ramifications were completely foreign, unknown to me. Questions have haunted me: *How could my son Jerry, a Christian, active in church, successful in business, well-loved and well-liked, become involved in the practice of homosexuality? How can a Christian be homosexual? Was Jerry controlled by the devil? Was Jerry mentally and emotionally sick and we did not know it? If even my son was homosexual and I did not recognize it, who else may I know that is practicing this lifestyle? Did I fail to nurture Jerry as his mother? Did Walter fail to fulfill his role as Jerry's father?* The questions go on.

I remember the moment I gathered my son Jerry in my arms, loved him, let him know that nothing mattered, assured him that I will be there to help him regardless. And I continue to feel the same way. I do love Jerry and I do thank God for letting me be his mother. I know that whatever comes, God will provide grace to see us through. There will be grace for me and Walter. Grace for Jerry. Grace for Terry, for Steve. And grace for our family members and friends.

For all those who love us and continue to pray for us, I thank God for you.

A grateful mother,

Clara Arterburn
January 29, 1988

Acknowledgments

The creation of this book has not been easy for anyone who was involved. I want to thank Victor Oliver, my publisher, for seeing the need for this book and caring enough for those who hurt to produce it. My able editor, Lila Empson, spent hours with me so she could accurately edit the book. She is a true professional and now a dear friend.

It has been difficult for my parents to have the secrets of our family opened up for public review. I am grateful for their courage that has allowed me to reach out to others. But I am most appreciative of their love that has been undying during these most difficult days. Their care and acceptance have been a wonderful gift from God.

My brothers and their wives have been a real source of strength to me. They have opened their homes to me and cared for me out of love. I am forever grateful for that love.

A special thanks to my younger brother, Steve, whose writing talent has allowed me to tell my story. Thank you for helping me help others.

To those thousands of prayer warriors from coast to coast who have fought for me, supported me, and encouraged me to carry on, my deepest gratitude.

HOW WILL I TELL MY MOTHER?

Part One

CHAPTER ONE

How Will I Tell My Mother?

I knew that something was very wrong. I anxiously awaited the doctor's visit that night. But even at that point I was not too worried. I had left the gay world behind me, and I felt that God had a plan for my life. I did not think that plan could include an early death.

That April evening in 1985, I lay in bed and stared at the ceiling while I awaited my doctor. I prayed that whatever the news, God would help me accept it and would allow me to use it in some way. Finally my doctor arrived accompanied by two others. It was apparent they were shaken. They were about to do something they were not adequately prepared to handle. I thought, *One doctor can deliver good news, and two can deliver bad news. So it must take three doctors to tell me that I will not survive.* Finally my doctor held onto my arm and looked down at me. "Jerry, I have some bad news for you that I wish I did not have to give you. There is a 99 percent chance that you have AIDS and that you will not recover from it."

The words sank in immediately. The big bad wolf had finally struck and had dealt me a death blow. I sank back in bed and looked up at the three men who were standing around me. One of the older men wiped a tear from his cheek. We all were suspended together in that most dark moment of reality. It was hard to believe that this was happening to me. I did not remember signing up to play the lead in a tragedy like this. I thought to myself that I had some things to do and I wanted the chance to do them. I looked straight into the eye of that doctor and said, "I'll take that 1 percent, and my God and I will defeat this thing." There were no tears from me. Only a smile from knowing that God would sustain me at my weakest state. As my power was made weak, I knew He would give me His strength. The doctors spent some more time with me and then left after telling me they would help me through this. Their care and concern were sincere.

After they left, I pulled out my Bible but couldn't read it. Some tears formed in my eyes as I began to think. *So this is how it is all going to end. I will have to go to my grave with a dark secret that no one must know.* Then I wondered if something good could come from all this. I realized that if I was to make my life count, eventually I would have to tell others of my ordeal. I couldn't make anything good come from my life by keeping it a secret. But I had programed myself to keep really big secrets from my family. For as long as possible, I decided I would not burden anyone else with my condition. Then a sinking feeling came into my stomach and filled my whole body. I envisioned an old picture of my parents that had been taken for the church directory. I thought of how good those two people were. They hadn't done anything to deserve going through something like this. It was too cruel for them.

I turned toward the dark window, calculating their

distance as but a few hundred miles outside it. I began to cry deeply. I, Jerry Arterburn, had become every parent's nightmare. I cried myself to sleep wondering, *How will I tell my mother?*

* * *

As I was growing up, I thought of Mother as a beautiful Christian woman who had to struggle most of her life. She struggled to raise her three sons in our modest Ranger, Texas, existence. She struggled with the untimely death of her father. And she struggled with our move from rural Ranger to the city of Bryan.

Mom was a model of what I thought moms were supposed to be. She was a provider of needs when we were young. She made sure we were fed three extra-delicious meals every day. And she made sure our home was a spotless place to bring friends. She dedicated her whole life to us. She was a giver, never asking much for herself. Her greatest thrills seemed to come from us boys and her participation in our pursuits.

No matter what the budget for clothes, Mother dressed us neatly in clothes that were always clean. I remember load after load going into the washer and dryer as my brothers and I did multiple clothes changes every day. And we never used the same towel two days in a row. Whatever Mother could do to make our lives better or easier, she gladly did it.

She was also our primary disciplinarian. At times our punishment would come from my father, but the sentence would have been pronounced by Mother. We always knew there were limits not to be crossed, and if we tested them it wouldn't be pleasant. Once Terry, my older brother, was instructed to hold a chocolate pie level in the car while en route to someone who was ill. My brother didn't manage to accomplish the goal, and before long chocolate pie had spilled on the seat and floorboard of the car. Mother calmly took the pie and put it all over Terry's face. The laughter at the entire incident came later.

I loved my mother deeply. She taught me and the others in the family how to laugh and how to care. She was a warm and loving person, and below the surface she had a fun-seeking streak just waiting to let loose.

Mom did love to laugh. She had a great sense of humor, and her friends counted on her to cut up and have a good time. Her wit helped all of us survive some rough times.

My mother was also a businesswoman. Although she believed in mothers staying at home to raise children, she also knew the needs of three boys going through college. So she purchased some beauty salons to manage. The money from those stores helped us with our college expenses. She would probably be some beauty salon mogul today if she hadn't developed an allergy to hair spray.

*   *   *

I jolted awake, my thoughts racing a thousand directions but converging on a single question, *How can I get out of this?* Fear and helplessness fastened like dead weights around my heart. There was no escape from the finality of my diagnosis.

Pneumocystis pneumonia, the doctor had said. I knew about pneumocystis pneumonia. When you've got pneumocystis, you've got AIDS, at least that's the way it seemed to work. Pneumocystis pneumonia signaled a deficiency in the immune system. Most people I knew about tested positive for AIDS before they developed pneumonia. They just started off feeling bad and feeling kind of sick, then they found out they had AIDS—and then they got pneumocystis pneumonia. That wasn't the way it was with me. No telling how long I'd had AIDS. I hadn't felt sick at all before I started running a 104° fever and went to the doctor for an x-ray.

I wished I could protect Mom from the hurt I knew I would cause. I wished I could erase the disappointment I knew she would feel. I thought about what a beautiful person she is and how she didn't deserve what I would put her through. I knew I would present her with her greatest struggle and challenge. I would bring this conservative, Christian woman face-to-face with any mother's worst fear. I would have to deliver the message to her that her homosexual son was dying of AIDS. I knew it would hit her hard and hurt her deeply, but I also knew she could take it. My mother is a survivor.

*   *   *

My family never had a lot of money. There wasn't enough money for me and my brothers to have an allowance, and so if we wanted any money to spend we had to earn it. My dad was in the oil-field machine and supply business and worked for his father at the shop just behind the house. He made enough money to feed us and keep us in clothes, but we had few luxuries. To have enough money for a vacation at the dude ranch in south Texas would rank as a miracle. In the early days our family's economy did not seem like an important issue to me, but looking back I realize how it affected the way I thought about other people. To me, someone with money was someone special. I was never able to eradicate the impact of those meager beginnings from my life. Although it produced within me a desire to better myself, it would also haunt me years later.

The little church in Ranger was where I first heard about God and Jesus and the three wise men. I had rolled underneath almost every pew and had explored the baptistery when it was drained of all its water. That church was good for little kids like me. I remember only remarkably caring people dedicated to teaching me God's truths, whether it was in Royal Ambassadors or Vacation Bible School. I learned how to sing "Jesus Loves Me" in Spanish. Even though I never sang the song to a Spanish person, I was grateful to have been made bilingual by the First Baptist Church.

Ranger is almost exactly between Fort Worth and Abilene, just off Interstate 30. About thirty-seven hundred people live there now, about forty-three hundred when we left. One of the local boys landed a starring role in *Jesus Christ Superstar,* and that was the most cosmopolitan event to happen in our little town. At the time we lived in Ranger, the streets were still made of red brick. And, indeed, there was only one traffic light, just at the edge of town by the railroad tracks. Ranger was the sort of idyllic place one would expect to find pictured in a book about small-town America. When we lived there, our family found few problems we could not handle. Ranger was a safe womb, tucked away from the outside world. Life there was simple and warm and loving. With the exceptions of watching the Ford dealership burn to the ground with about ten cars still in it and running to the storm shelter to avoid being swept up in a tornado, my childhood in Ranger was without fear.

Our first house was just down the road about a

quarter of a mile from the church. My family and I walked that red-brick road twice on almost every Sunday and once on almost every Wednesday. There were exceptions to that rule. We would drive if there was inclement weather or if we had purchased a new car the previous week. I do not ever remember more than one or two new cars purchased while living in Ranger, and so that exception would have been very rare. But I do remember loading up in a new yellow Mercury to make the quarter-mile drive on a perfectly sunny day. I was quite proud of that car.

Our place was centrally located. We were close to the church, and the only thing more important than church in our town was football—and we lived directly across the street from the stadium. In addition, there was an O.K. grocery store just behind the house and across the main drag. It was an ideal location. The school I attended was, at most, a five-minute walk. I always thought that if I ever had kids they would not respect me because I wouldn't be able to tell them I had trudged through ten miles of snow to attend school like all of the grown-ups I respected had. But it was wonderful to be so close to so many things that were important to our small town.

We lived about as close as we could to my grandparents. Our little five-room house, my grandparents' house, and my grandfather's machine shop were all located on the same lot. Terry and Steve and I were raised by my parents and my grandparents. I loved being next door to my grandmother. Everyone called her Mother Art. Whenever we would shoot a sparrow with a BB gun, we could hardly wait to go show our prize game to the matriarch of the Arterburn family. I don't think we believed she had some weird love to see dead animals, but we had witnessed the ritual so many times. The men of the family, my dad and his four brothers, would drive up to the back door with a truckload of dead ducks or quail or dove or pheasant and hold them up and grin while the women would look on with admiration. It was kind of like a dead-bird-of-the-month club. Although our sparrows were not edible, we must have felt we had accomplished something worthy of admiration by shooting the life out of those little sparrows. (When I heard Ethel Waters sing "His Eye Is on the Sparrow," I thought to myself that God must have overlooked those we blew out of the trees with our BB guns from the Western Auto on Main Street.)

My grandmother was more than just a surveyor of dead game animals. She was and still is a fantastic lady. There is no fonder memory than that of sitting out on the front porch of her little house, eating ice-cold watermelon, and spitting out the seeds on her lawn. She made an extra effort to make each one of her grandchildren feel special. I loved it when, after making a batch of pies, she would give me my own special pie made in an individual Swanson's chicken pot pie pan. No one could cook like she could, and no one will ever be able to cook like she could, because she put herself into it. The love she cooked into her food made it a work of art. But we admired her for more than her cooking. We loved her because of who she was and the character she was made of. My grandfather was not always at his best. He was a Texan's Texan, with plans of his own and a design for marriage that would probably give Gloria Steinem a stroke. But his manner never seemed to bother Mother Art. She was as patient and kind to him as anyone could be. She was a living example of the love of Christ being funneled through one person to another. For the sake of all the little ones growing up today, I sure hope they make grandmothers like they used to. Mine certainly added meaning to my early life.

We lived in Ranger until my ninth year. The summers there were always a lot of fun. Each year our family entered a crepe paper–decorated wagon in the Fourth of July parade. My brothers, Terry (three years older) and Steve (three years younger), and I spent most of our summers running around with baseball caps on our heads. Dad coached our Little League team. I was a fairly good player until I stood in the wrong place while Terry was taking batting practice. He swung his bat as hard as he could—and the end of that bat thrust sideways into my very fragile nose. My pain registered about a 9.9 on the Richter scale. No one has ever known pain like that kind of pain. Terry's swing put a natural curve in my nose and closed off one passage entirely. Years later, corrective surgery would undo the damage, but that accident practically ruined my baseball career. It was a long time before I could relax when someone started swinging a bat.

Life in the beginning was nothing less than wonderful. We didn't have a lot of luxuries, but we didn't know it. Or at least we had no feelings of inferiority because of our modest beginnings. Although we had so limited means, Mom and Dad were best friends with the Guests (Wilson Guest was president of the bank and one of the wealthier people in town), and we went on vacation trips with them. That was important to me because I respected them so much. Their example made me strive to achieve beyond my current circumstances.

The banker's son and my brother Terry had a joint FFA (Future Farmers of America) project of raising sheep. The intent was to learn ranching and make some money (which never occurred). We had moved into a house at the edge of a hill, and the large yard to the side of the house was perfect for a sheep pen. One day while my mother and D. J. (the banker's wife) were having coffee, the sheep escaped from their pen and proceeded up the hill behind our house. The hill was in plain view of most of the residences below in the town. Mother and D. J. went racing up the hill, each with a turquoise hula-hoop to round up the sheep. But the more they tried to round them up, the further the sheep scattered. Finally the people down below saw the turquoise hoops and the sheep, and they started gathering around the house and up on the hill to assist in the roundup. The whole escapade was written up in the *Ranger Times* the following week. Not long thereafter, the sheep were sold at a substantial loss to all of us.

The winters of my youth brought their own joy with them. I can remember snow deep enough to make footprints and snowmen (or snowwomen, since we never made gender distinctions). My dad would hook a sleigh behind my grandfather's pickup truck and pull us all over town. And when we rounded a corner, it was a challenge just to hang on. We were the luckiest kids in town because no one else had a big sleigh like ours. More laughter came out of that sleigh than from a Bill Cosby audience. And if the sleigh was out and running, it always meant that Christmas was not far away.

Christmas was such a warm and loving time. When I think about our Christmases, I can almost feel shivers of emotion on the back of my neck. Each year about thirty of us packed into my grandparents' small house for a grand celebration. We ate more than could normally be consumed and then gathered around a huge tree to open presents.

At Christmas, Dad Art would always cry for joy at having his family with him. He cried at other times, too. Each day he came home for lunch and lay down to watch *As the World Turns*. He often cried while watching the same plot retold from a previous season. But it was always a good bet that he would cry at Christmas. He would do other things, too. Unlike my teetotaling Southern Baptist father, Dad Art was a drinker. Each year he would produce his own recipe of eggnog—with plenty of "nog," as he put it. When my parents weren't around, he encouraged us to have a little sip with him. If my father had found out, I'm sure he would have washed my mouth out with soap.

I will never forget the Christmas when Dad Art wanted to create the illusion that Santa and his reindeer were pulling up outside. We kids were all in bed when he yelled that Santa had arrived. Snow and ice blanketed the lawn, and Dad Art—clothed only in his underwear—circled the house jingling bells as he went. When we heard Dad Art's yell, we all sat straight up in bed and listened. The sleigh bells were ringing just outside the window! At that moment whatever doubts we had about the existence of Santa were wiped away. We knew there was a Santa because he was out on our lawn.

We would probably still believe that today if the illusion had not been destroyed by my grandmother. We heard her yell, "Art, get back in the house with your underwear on or you'll freeze to death. And quit ringing those bells so loud. You're going to wake the entire town!" We knew we had been the victims of a master deception, but we loved Dad Art for it anyway.

*   *   *

Thinking back to those times of a packed house full of relatives and the smell of a gas stove burning in a lime green bathroom, I found myself fighting back the deep desire to go back to those days and do my life over. If I allowed myself to dwell on the "If Only's," I would do nothing but intensify my misery. What might have been could be no more. I had to reckon with the battle for my life. Feeling regret or looking back could lessen my chance for survival.

A wave of mixed emotions washed over me as I looked at Tony, my companion and friend. We had lived together for only about six months. Now he was visiting me in the hospital. His back was slightly turned, his eyes staring out the window. *Is he afraid?* There had been some good times together. Whenever Tony and I had gone out, we'd put on starched shirts and jeans and boots. We looked very sharp and clean. When people saw us, they knew we were together. It was an exhilarating feeling. But our six months together hadn't been all good. I hadn't been fair to Tony or to myself or to God, and now my ambivalence would hurt the people I cared about and cost me my life.

The irony of my diagnosis is that just a year and a half earlier I had given up the homosexual lifestyle and had lived a complete year celibate; I hadn't wanted anything to do with the gay world. During that year I wrestled with the life I had lived and the life I wanted to live. But I had tried to break away on my own, and the effort proved too difficult. I was still vacillating between the excitement that had attracted me to gay life and the peace I thought I could find in straight life. I had even begun investigating the possibility of going to seminary. I wanted more than the "good" life. I wanted the *good* life.

It was hard to believe that I, of all people, an honor graduate of a major university in Texas, a born-again Christian, active in the Southern Baptist denomination, could have knowingly entered the world of homosexuality and contracted the deadly AIDS virus. I had taught Sunday school and had even preached from the pulpit. I had dated some wonderful women. I had never had a sexual relationship of any kind until I was twenty-seven. I had lived a clean and chaste life. But for most of my life I had battled the desires that I knew were wrong. Then at the very time that I made my final decision to leave the gay world and rededicate my life to Christ, I was confronted with the worst. It was a nightmare, and I would have to live out its entirety, waking from it only when I cross over into the promised land.

The decision was easier this time. No more vacillating, no more ambivalence. I would still care for Tony as a dear friend, but I was out of the gay life. Period. I left the hospital a little more than a week later, and I was determined to make what was left of my life count. Tony said he understood, and we parted friends.

The next weeks and months blurred into a maze of alternating activity and fatigue. I was successful in breaking away from the physical presence of my homosexual past, but dealing with its consequences in the present was far too distressing. I thought often about suicide, and I mentally rehearsed how I would do it. Suicide seemed to be a way out of the dilemma I was in.

*   *   *

I was four years old when my grandfather on my mother's side committed suicide. He was named Roy Russell, and my middle name was Laroy after him. His job was stressful, and he experienced great mood swings. Earlier in his life he had been a gentle and kind man and had been involved in every imaginable activity. In the last few months before his death, however, he had been a completely different person. He would break into outbursts of rage followed by long times of seclusion.

Some people thought that since his behavior was so bizarre, perhaps he had a brain tumor. His depressions became so severe that he was admitted to a Dallas psychiatric hospital for electroshock therapy. At the time, no anesthesia was administered before the convulsion-inducing currents penetrated the brain. When he was released, he never seemed to get better. And he knew the family was planning on putting him back in the hospital for more treatments. So he took a shotgun and mounted it under the muffler and the gas tank of the car and crawled under so that the barrel fit close to his mouth. Then he pulled the trigger and took his life.

It was a devastating blow to our family and the entire community. My grandfather was a fine Christian man who was loved by many. But he had done something that was unacceptable. His manner of death—suicide—had a stigma attached to it. There were those who thought if you died by suicide you could not be a Christian and you certainly would not go to heaven. The effect of his death on my mother was profound. She was deeply depressed over the loss of her father, and her loss was accompanied by profound embarrassment that he committed suicide. The suicide was kept secret as much as possible. In fact, my younger brother Steve did not know it was suicide until he was in high school and Terry told him. The secrecy hurt. It prevented me from resolving the questions that surrounded the suicide. As I grew older, I realized I could not trust adults to be immortal, nor could I trust them to tell me the truth.

After my grandfather died, I watched my grandmother deal with his death over the years. She didn't grow bitter toward God, as others might have; she didn't succumb to self-pity. She grew in her faith in God. In fact, her faith became stronger, her attitude more positive, as she faced the difficulties of living alone. She was an inspiration to those around her. In every conversation, she talked about how good God is or how wonderful heaven is going to be.

*   *   *

It was a real temptation to go the way of the man I was named for. I, like my grandfather, had a problem that Christians are not supposed to experience and a condition that many think Christians would never develop. There is a theory that if a member of your family has committed suicide you are at greater risk than someone from a family where suicide is unknown. It doesn't likely become a method of death if it hasn't been used by someone close. It occurred to me that my grandfather's death by suicide was what was making me consider it so often as a way out of my dilemma. I decided to postpone my death because I realized that if it were delayed, I could create something of value from my mistakes. If I took my life, it would only add to the trauma that I had brought to my family and others that are close.

I determined to model the faith of my grandmother. And I determined to capture her will to persevere in the midst of adversity. I reached out for her faith because I knew mine was weak. She had no idea how she was helping me survive. God always allows something good to come of the tragedies in our lives, and with my grandfather's early death, God could make much value come from it.

*   *   *

My grandfather Roy's death left three very important male figures in my life: Dad, Dad Art, and Terry. Our little town was safe, but not always safe and warm for me. I feared these three males to some degree. In an angry tirade, my grandfather once kicked me with his boots on. He kicked me in the head. I could never forget that. I couldn't be near him unless I thought of the horrible blow from his boot and the sight of my blood. My father never hit me like that, but he did whip me and my brothers with a board or belt until it hurt. I know that if Dad had it to do over, he would not be so physical with his punishment, but at the time he didn't know any better. His father had raised him that way. But his punishments made me afraid to make any mistakes or even come home late from school. Most of my drive to be a perfectionist must have come from the fear of my father's board and belt, because I didn't want to be the victim of that much pain on a regular basis. Being hit so regularly probably caused some of the violence between me and my older brother. Terry had a temper and would hit me, perhaps modeling what my father had done, or perhaps seeking displaced revenge upon my father by hurting me. I in turn would be violent with Steve. The result was that very early in life I was afraid of the three men closest to me. And that fear led to a sense of alienation from most other males I met. I wanted to be accepted by them, but I also was afraid of pain and rejection.

The fear I felt at home led me to love school more than most kids. Mrs. Barret and Mrs. McDaniels were great to me at the little elementary school in Ranger. I was Mrs. Barret's pet, but she and Mrs. McDaniels both took an extraordinary interest in me. They thought I was talented. And so did the other kids. During the Thanksgiving play production, the others wanted me to paint the turkeys and make the hats. And I was proud to do it, too. The care from those teachers, and the warmth I felt from the old radiators, made school a favorite place for me. It was a place where I could excel, and I did just that. It was more than just a place for safety; it was a place where I could be somebody. Even as early as third grade, I worked hard to have a better life. From the beginning, I was determined to be somebody and use my talents to get ahead.

I used other ways to get ahead, too. I felt driven in my quest for something better. I entered the world of commerce through the establishment of a Kool-Aid stand that sold iced cold Kool-Aid for five cents a cup. I went from that enterprise to sharing a paper route at the age of six with Terry. My brother and I were able to save enough money from that route to buy our own motor scooter. I wanted to stand out, and making money of my own allowed me to do that. As far back as I can remember, I needed to be distinctive and set apart from the crowd.

It wasn't a totally selfish desire to accomplish things above what was expected. I wanted to do it for the entire family. I felt that I was the one child that could stand out and grow up to be something. I believed that I would be the shining star of the family and that I would bring value to us all. I didn't know whether it would be by my becoming president of the United States or one of the world's greatest artists; I just knew I had a desire to do great things that my friends didn't have. Nor did I want to live in that little town all of my life. I wanted to do as my uncles had done and move on to bigger and better places.

When my father received confirmation that he had been given the job he wanted in Bryan, Texas, we were all thrilled. But we were also sad to leave our friends behind—and afraid we wouldn't like the new place. The thought of not fitting in plagued us. Those fears proved to be grounded in reality. When we pulled out of Ranger after a royal send-off, our lives were never the same. A world of opportunity opened up for us. But with the opportunity for us to have a better life also came the exposure to some of the dangers that hadn't seemed to exist back in Ranger. Each of us in our own way had great difficulty with the move. It's hard not to look back and wonder whether it was the best or worst move we would ever make. It isn't easy to keep from wondering what might have been and what might not have been had we stayed in Ranger, our little womb away from the world.

CHAPTER TWO

An Alienated Adolescent

The move to Bryan, Texas, population sixty thousand, was a disaster I didn't know whether we would endure. The entire four and a half hours it took to drive there from Ranger, my mother spent crying. You would have thought my dad had kidnapped her and was taking her to a forbidden land against her will. Well, in a sense maybe he was. She hated the thought of leaving her best friends and having to make new ones. In Ranger she felt like a fairly good size fish in a small pond. In Bryan she would be smaller than a minnow in an ocean of people she didn't know. She said she couldn't imagine going to the grocery store and not being able to charge a loaf of bread or know anyone in the entire store. Whatever the real source of her dread, her emotional resistance certainly made it hard for the rest of us to have warm feelings about the place. And since she had already been there a couple of times and had picked out our house, we thought the place must be awfully rotten.

Once we arrived, things didn't turn immediately for the better. I was quite thrilled at the new house we rented—it looked like a very nice neighborhood (whatever one of those was)—but the weather couldn't have been worse. For at least ninety days and ninety nights it did nothing but rain and rain and then let up and rain some more. I was afraid to walk out on our front lawn for fear I would sink right down and never be heard from again. The military should have issued rain gear to everyone who entered Bryan. It was a key to survival. And the humidity that preceded and followed the rain storms was something that made us all suffer. Before Bryan I didn't know what a sinus was, but after only a few days I learned all about them because I was attacked by mine and the other family members were also attacked by theirs. We were all in pain from the worst imaginable headaches, and common aspirin couldn't knock them out. We must have been a miserable family to be around because we were sure a miserable family to be in. It is a wonder that my dad didn't just pack us all up and take us back to Ranger. (My mother's crying didn't stop until after the rain did.)

In Bryan there was a thing called "civility." The ladies had coffees and teas for each other. It was all very fancy when someone had a party. Parties were more than just getting out the charcoal and barbecuing a goat. Bryan was a completely different environment. The people were very difficult to get used to. The first Sunday night we were there we all went over to my dad's boss's house after church for a little "fellowship," as they called it. I just didn't fit in with those people. While the kids played out back, all the adults stayed in the house and talked. It was somewhat like a debut for my mom and dad, but for me it was a catastrophe. No sooner had we chosen up sides for football than some twins (who would for the next several years be held up to my brothers and me as model children) tackled me to the ground for no apparent reason at all. I felt embarrassed and hurt. So approximately five minutes into my first encounter with Bryanites, I headed for the car to sit out the rest of the evening. Our car had some big fins on the back, and I thought, *If I could drive, I could back the car into all of them and commit mass fin murder by stacking them up as I throttled down in reverse.* It was a good thing my dad had the keys to the car. I thought to myself that it was no wonder that mother had cried all the way here. She had been here before, and she knew that the people were cruel. At least, that's how I interpreted her tears. Not more than thirty seconds after I had that thought, I saw the front door open. My mother came out to the car, wiping the tears from her eyes, and I could tell things hadn't gone well for her either. She sat there a while, comforted me, and then went back in. But there was no way I was going to return to those bullies in the back. The next thing I remember was being carried in my own house by my father. He thought I was asleep, and I allowed him to think it. It had been a bad night for me, and I wanted no part of the people that lived there.

The following day I had to go to school for the first time at Crockett Elementary (named after Davy Crockett), home of the Crockett Rockets. The school song was hanging on the wall, and it went something like this: "We are the Crockett Rockets, the Rockets from Crockett are we. We'll go so far and brighten every star, and then zoom onto victory!" *Dumb song,* I thought. It was posted in the hall just outside the principal's office where I was going to report with my mother and older brother. All I wanted to do was to zoom out of that school. But after Mom filled out a bunch of papers, the counselor took me to my class. The last thing on earth I wanted to do was to stand up in front of a class of thirty strangers as mean as the kids from the night before and be introduced as the new kid in town. I felt unwanted and rejected. There I stood as the counselor told the class that I was from Ranger and would be completing the year with them. There was total silence, and then a kid named Jess Burditt stood up and said, "Well at least we got another boy this time." Everyone laughed. I didn't know what he meant, but I knew how I felt—humiliated.

*   *   *

Those initial events in Bryan planted a feeling of rejection that grew into a feeling of dislocation. I simply was in the wrong place. I was an alien. And I continued to feel that way for most of my days in that school and that town. It's hard for me to sort out the way I felt, and only now was I able to begin to do so. As the feelings of insecurity grew and the feelings of alienation built up, I developed some urges I didn't understand. I wanted acceptance from those who rejected me. I became aware of an increasing desire to be close to other boys. It was "just a phase" (or so I thought), and I didn't let it worry me too much. But I was in a bind. I felt rejection at the same time I wanted affection. And I didn't want affection from relatives. I avoided their hugs and kisses—I thought they were germy. I craved attention and acceptance of another kind, and I battled those feelings as early as the third grade.

But my feelings about other boys and the alienation I felt hadn't just "appeared" in third grade. I trace that back to a traumatic experience I had at the age of five. If you are going to understand how I became trapped—and how others become trapped—you must not overlook experiences similar to the one I had at church camp in Ludders, Texas.

*   *   *

I had convinced the youth leader (at least my brother had) that I was mature enough to go to camp. So he let me go with my parents' permission. It was a great adventure at first. I loved being with the older kids and acting grown up.

One evening after hearing the camp preacher tell about the prodigal son, as we all sat out under the stars, I experienced a tremendous feeling of love, and I began to weep. I thought of the love Jesus has for all of us, and I was determined not to be mean to my parents like the boy who went to live with the pigs. That night I asked Jesus to come into my heart (although I did not make it public until I was sixteen). I had a wonderful Christian experience and felt very close to God. I felt as light as a helium-filled balloon. It was great to be alive.

But later that night, all those incredible, spiritual feelings were destroyed. After the lights went out and everyone had gone to bed, I fell asleep but was awakened by one of the older boys. He put his finger to his mouth to hush me. Then he told me he wanted to make me feel grown up, and so he was going to let me do some things that grown-ups did. He said that I must never tell anyone and that if I did, he would come into my house one night, wrap me in a sheet, and carry me to the cemetery where he would bury me alive. Then he took my hand and placed it on his genital. He guided my hands to touch him so he would feel good. I knew with all of my heart that it was wrong, but it made me feel something I could not understand. When he left, I was confused and hurt and sick thinking about what had happened. I cried silently in my pillow until I fell asleep.

The next morning when I awoke, I felt the heaviness of guilt like I had never felt it before. And I could say nothing to anyone for fear of being dragged out to some cemetery to die. But I wouldn't have told anyone anyway. It was too embarrassing. I didn't know how a person talked about those kinds of things. I couldn't look anyone in the eye. I looked down at the ground for fear someone would detect what I had done by looking into the depths of my eyes. I was so ashamed. And it was such a drastic change from the good feeling I'd had when only the night before I had sat under the stars and felt God's presence so close.

*　*　*

That night lit the fuse that derailed my desires. I was a victim of sexual abuse, and my victimization was, literally, the beginning of the end.

Even though I was only five at the time, I knew not to talk about my experience ("good little boys don't . . .")—in fact, my sense of having done something wrong probably tinged my experience with the exciting overlay of the forbidden. Of course, no one had specifically warned me about homosexuality. How many parents talk about *any* kind of sex with their preschoolers?

My struggle for the past thirty or so years is similar to that of many other male homosexuals I have met who were molested or introduced to homosexual behavior by older boys or men. That first encounter, ironically, supplied me with the male attention I craved at the same time it nibbled away at my already shaky feelings of strength and security. When I later went through adolescence, I needed more than the normal share of attention and nurturing to help me get through the transitions. When I didn't get what I needed emotionally, I felt devastated. I sought comfort in my dreams to compensate for the feelings of emptiness that had become my companion.

Early experiences with older persons are a key to the development of homosexual behavior. I place this factor as the link between normal and abnormal development. Shrouded in secrecy and shame, they affect future relationships and desires. I am not attempting to blame anyone for my problems—I later was the one to make some very poor decisions—but the experience of early exposure to homosexual behavior is quite common among many homosexuals I have known. Often children do not even know that touching or being touched is wrong because they have no one to talk to about the incident. The value of the recent child abuse cases making the headlines is that it may encourage parents to take precautions so that their children are warned about child molesters. Parents must tell their children that no one has the right to touch them on the parts covered up by a bathing suit. And children need to know they are safe in telling the parent anything. Children must feel there will be protection, not condemnation.

*   *   *

Moving to Bryan and feeling detached from the other kids caused my desire for male affection to escalate. I talked to no one about it. My grandfather's suicide and the hush-hush circumstances left me with the impression that some things were best not discussed. I became more self-conscious and grew more aloof. I buried myself in schoolwork. I hid in my achievements. Whenever there was a report or a project to be done, I went to work on it sooner and worked harder than the others. I was driven to be the best. If I could not feel the same as the others around me, I wanted to prove I could be superior. It was my way of coping with being uncomfortable and feeling like an outcast.

My self-consciousness grew into an obsession. I wanted people to see me only at my best. I spent hours in the bathroom checking and rechecking my appearance. I sought perfection even in the way I looked, and there were things I didn't want anyone to see or know. I didn't want anyone to see me without my shirt. I swam and water-skied with my T-shirt on. I was embarrassed because I had matured early and my body was covered with more hair than the other boys my age. I didn't like myself very much, and despite my talent and intelligence, my self-esteem was very low. I wished we had never left Ranger. I wanted to somehow get out of the noose that I knew was starting to strangle me.

My discomfort continued through the years of elementary and junior high school. I was a loner in many respects and avoided getting close to anyone. I especially grew distant from my family. I rarely talked at dinner and found ways not to be around my parents and brothers. I told them that they didn't know me. I told them I was a different person when I was away from the house. I was angry. I blamed my parents for my not fitting in. But instead of telling them that, I bowed out of the role they would have had me play. They wanted me to be a good little boy and obey the rules. I thought their rules were foolish. They told me not to drink or smoke, and I thought it was ridiculous to discuss smoking or drinking when I felt so bad about just being me. At times I wanted to scream out that I needed help. I wanted to tell them they didn't understand me because they had no idea how confused and hurt I was on the inside. The anger they saw was a mask.

My confusion was rooted in increasing doubts about who I was and who I was becoming. I was scared to death that I either was becoming gay or was gay already. I craved the attention of men and guys my age. I felt safe and whole when other males paid attention to me. Females made me feel just the opposite—I wasn't attracted to any of them. I felt queasy being close to a girl because I feared her ridicule and rejection. But the prospect of being close to another boy was different. I wondered just how weird I was. I didn't know enough about homosexuality to know what I actually had to do to be a homosexual or how close I was to the condition. I lived behind a self-depressing mask of secrecy, and I especially hid my fears from my family. I didn't want them to suspect I was anything but tough and hard and strong. My goal was to keep this terrible secret a secret—forever. The stronger my fears, the more impenetrable my mask became.

I wore a mask around others, also. In high school no one had any idea I was anything but normal and happy. Because I was talented and had what I believed to be a good sense of humor, I had quite a few friends. But it wasn't fun for me because of how I felt about myself and others. In a Texas town full of "red necks" and "goat ropers," boys just didn't talk about their emotions.

Some nights the other guys and I would ride around together. On the outside I was good at playing the part of a guy out to find a girl, but on the inside I was afraid we might actually find some girls and ask them to go riding with us. When everyone else wanted to kiss and hug, I tried to do anything else but that. But I never told anyone how I felt. I kept it all to myself.

*　*　*

I wish now that I had gone for counseling. It would have been a major help and perhaps might have turned things around when I was very young. But I thought then that going to counseling was a sign of weakness. Now I know it was my weakness that *prevented* me from going. Discussing my problems with no one, I didn't know where to turn or what to do. So I just continued in emotional turmoil, alone.

*　*　*

I learned to do one thing to ease my pain—drink. It was the only thing I did more of than study. A crowd wasn't so threatening when I had a few drinks. But it was rarely a few drinks. I drank a lot of beer with the guys. The weeks when I was the most anguished and frustrated were the weeks I drank the most. To my friends, a beer in my hand was a common sight. I saw no harm in the drinking. It was fun and also comforting. My parents warned against it, my Southern Baptist church preached against it, but I didn't pay any attention. Perhaps the warnings made the drinking more enticing. Whatever the allure, once I started drinking, I rarely stopped before I had drunk at least a six-pack of beer. When the six-pack was in my system, the frustration and guilt lost their intensity. The alcohol took the edge off the pain. I had no idea how dangerous that behavior was.

Drinking wasn't the only behavior the church was against. The church also informed all its young that dancing—couples dancing—led to problems. I thought those teachings, like the ones against drinking, were just intended to prevent me and everyone else from having a good time. The "old folks" resented the young folks really enjoying themselves. Dancing was one thing that I loved to do with a girl. Fast dancing, that is. When I danced, and I danced pretty well, I felt freedom. It allowed me to escape into an enchanted land of colored lights, dim lights, beats, rhythms, movement, and excitement. To me if there was anything wrong with dancing, it was that not enough people knew how to do it well.

*   *   *

Looking back, I hate to admit how "right on target" the teachings had been. The theory of the fundamental church is that passion and desire are stirred up as two people move closely together. The dance is the preliminary step toward fornication, especially for young, emotional teenagers. The combination of drinking and dancing led me to and kept me in places I had no business being. I didn't see it then, but those places where I felt at ease were the places where I was farthest from God and His will for my life. There is nothing good about escaping into a world where the spiritual values are left out—and the world of drink and the world of dance are two such places. Those two places of spiritual avoidance desensitized me to times away from God.

When I later entered into the homosexual lifestyle, it wasn't such a large leap.

Having the upbringing I had, I was warned about the problems that can develop from moving out from under God's protection. But I resented the church. I rebelled against it and what it stood for. I felt it was a hypocritical society of politics and power. I didn't have pleasant experiences associated with such a society. The first homosexual advance came at a church camp and the second came at a church function. One of the unmarried male choir members at our Bryan church grabbed my crotch while we were on an outing. It repulsed me. I ran from him and avoided him from that day forward. The experience only lasted five seconds, but it led me to doubt the authenticity of the church's teachings. That "dirty old man" sat in the choir in front of everyone, professing to be a Christian, yet look what he did to young boys. I could understand the evil outside the church, but not the evil within. I didn't understand that Christians still have major problems even after their conversion. I didn't understand that Christ died for the imperfect. I didn't understand that accepting Christ does not produce perfection. I was idealistic, and that choir member's homosexual advance shattered the ideal church for me.

There was yet another incident that helped shape my doubt. Our preacher, who had earned a doctor of theology degree, was held in high regard within the Southern Baptist denomination. And I respected him, also. I thought he represented everything good and wonderful about the Christian life. All that changed one Sunday. When he concluded his sermon, the church deacons passed out a letter of resignation. It was a shock to the whole congregation. Some superfluous statements were made, but the real reasons for the sudden departure weren't revealed—not then, anyway. The real reason came later, when the rumor mill ground out the news that our preacher (by then former preacher) was leaving his wife of some twenty years. Not long after the divorce was final, the more shocking news hit that he was going to marry a recently widowed woman from the church. And the woman was a good friend of my mother!

I was shaken over that event. It seemed that I could trust no one or believe in anything I had been taught. The people who were supposed to be the closest to God, who were supposed to represent the relationship we are to have with God, proved to be "just like all the rest." So when I doubted my faith, I doubted big. And my doubts led me to abandon what the church taught. I lost all reverence for the church and took nothing as gospel. I tried to figure out life, values, meaning, and right and wrong on my own. I thought I was intelligent enough to know how to live. The church, in my mind, was not doing much to help those closest to it figure out how to live their lives.

The church may have been more important for me than for most because Mom and Dad were so dedicated to it. Dad was the closest thing to being a minister without actually being one. He served on just about every committee and council that had been established. Our family's relationship to the church was not a casual one. We were a committed group, and much of our lives revolved around it. I believed that God favored the Southern Baptists over people of other denominations and certainly over other religions. I thought that *real* Christians were Southern Baptists—we were all right and everyone else was all wrong. At least that's what I thought until the actions of the choir member and the preacher led me to conclude that we were *not* all right and that some members were all wrong. Things got so distorted for me that I abandoned the church's teachings in favor of my personal rationalizations. My behavior in the years that followed went against Scripture, church, and family.

*   *   *

As I finished my high-school years, I developed my own standards. When it came to Christian behavior, my standards always allowed for something less than godly. But all my standards weren't bad. I had learned early what excellence meant, and I attempted to achieve it in everything I did. As a member of the tennis team, I was never satisfied with good effort—I wanted a win. I spent hours trying to perfect each painting and sketch. I achieved straight *A*'s. My lonely hours at home, studying and perfecting my projects, allowed me to attain the level of excellence I desired. The long hours allowed me to isolate myself from a difficult world, and I enjoyed the time for superior achievement. I "proved" that if anyone was going to save our family, if anyone was going to bring recognition and pride to our name, it would be me. My standard was a cut above, and everything I did was an effort to see just how much I could accomplish.

When I graduated, my entry in the yearbook was full of organizations I had been in and honors I had won. It didn't contain any reference to the disillusionment I felt about my life. I didn't consider myself homosexual, but I felt different, incomplete, and in need of something I didn't understand. The yearbook didn't explain how during my high-school days the church had produced more doubts than answers, doubts that led me away from church and toward situations I couldn't handle. My spiritual growth mirrored the distortions of my goals and priorities. I moved away from honoring God and toward honoring myself. I continued to compile personal honors through four years of college, four years of looking stronger on the outside while growing weaker within.

CHAPTER THREE

All-American College Boy

When I finally set off for college, I only had to travel five miles from my front door. Texas A&M University was just a short drive to the next town of College Station. I had had dreams of going away to Texas Tech in Lubbock or to Texas University in Austin, but we couldn't afford it. One semester at A&M only cost me about a hundred and fifty dollars, and so in the beginning I had to live at home and drive out to school each day. I felt confined living at home and began working and saving so that I could move into an apartment as soon as possible. I was not happy about having to go to A&M, but I realized I was fortunate to be able to attend a university with such a fine architectural school.

The key to my decision to attend Texas A&M was not only its cost, but also its School of Architecture. I wanted to be a world-renowned architect, and A&M could help me achieve my dream. While in high school I had done well in drafting and was recognized as a potential talent in the realm of architecture. For a perfectionist like me, architecture was an ideal area of study.

Architecture is a world of the precise, an art of the predictable. I was fascinated by lines, points, edges, and shapes. I could always count on what I constructed or designed to be nothing more or nothing less. I was never disappointed. I could make a perfect house with perfect walls and windows. I was able to create something bigger than myself that I hoped someone would discover and eventually construct. The time I spent working on even the simplest cardboard models and projects made me feel a little immortal. I was doing something that would remain after I had gone. It was wonderful to do something I loved in every way. While other students were complaining about the rigors of their studies, I was having the time of my life. I felt good about me.

I spent hours and hours on projects while I was in school. Evenings and weekends were often packed with nothing but long hours of creating and perfecting designs. Even when I moved out of my parents' house I continued to work hard rather than get distracted with the freedom of living away from home. My roommate was an architect student, also, and he joined me in the long hours of study. He was a decent guy, and his self-discipline complemented mine. His willingness to work hard motivated me to work even harder. I admired him greatly.

During the entire time I lived with him, I had little problem with my abnormal feelings. The first year with him set me on a normal path during the initial college years. I no longer had thoughts about being homosexual. In fact, I thought many times my feelings had only been a stage I had gone through and that I was really quite normal, or something very close. I sensed I was making progress because I no longer sought out or was attracted to male affection.

Texas A&M was not a fun place to go to school. My initial goal was to obtain a degree as quickly as possible and move. I did manage to find some things other than schoolwork, however, that I enjoyed very much. During those days I really wanted to date girls, but my school had about four boys to every girl (it had once been an all-boys military school). So I, like many other "Aggies," traveled ninety miles north to Baylor University in Waco, Texas. Baylor was known for its beautiful girls. They had a special look about them, and they represented decency and goodness. It was the kind of place a boy from Texas would want to visit in search of the perfect wife. I went there to find the perfect date and a few hours of escape. The trip was short, but it was far enough that I could put Bryan behind me. I felt like a real college student on the Baylor campus, and my adventures there were always exciting. When I would end up with a cute girl who appreciated a good dancer, I felt like a king. My college experience was certainly not typical for someone struggling with sexual identity problems. It was closer to a picture of the all-American boy.

One night I traveled to Baylor to have a date with an attractive girl from Bryan named Connie Reed. She was a great Christian girl, and I was thrilled to go out with her. All the way up I kept thinking what a special evening it was going to be. I had no idea how right I was. When I arrived, I watched couple after couple come down the steps of the dormitory as I pulled into the parking lot. I considered myself fortunate to be in a place like that while some of my friends were dying half-way around the world in Vietnam. I felt so privileged. I thought I was set apart and that God was protecting me from the hardships of the world. I believed I was invincible. I parked the car and sauntered up the steps of the dorm with great pride. I had come to conquer! I rang up to Connie's room and her roommate answered, saying that Connie would be right down. I nervously waited for her in the lobby.

Seconds later this loud and incredibly beautiful girl came rushing up to me, smiling over the most beautiful teeth as she told me that I must be Jerry. She was Connie's roommate, Martha Logan. She was full of life and energy. She didn't have a timid cell or a shy particle in her body. I liked her immediately, and I think she liked me, too. She was the daughter of a missionary couple who were in Enugu, Nigeria. Her father was a dentist and was helping the natives there while bringing them the gospel. It was so admirable that they had sacrificed their lives and she, being without parents to raise her, had also had to sacrifice. That, I believe, was the source of her independent nature. We talked for a while, and by the time Connie came down I realized how much I really liked Martha. But my date was with Connie. After we left Martha, I set out to discover as much as possible about the missionary's daughter. The evening was fun, but I spent most of it wondering how I could politely switch from dating one roommate to dating the other.

The assertive young lady I met that night took care of the dilemma for me. She told Connie when she arrived home from our date that she wanted to go out with me. Connie agreed that would be fine since we were just friends and expected nothing to come of our relationship. By the time I approached the subject with Connie, it had all been arranged. Martha and I planned our first evening together to be the annual Ring Ball at A&M. When I picked her up, I thought she was beautiful. She wore a long dress that accented her great figure. I was proud to be seen with her. That night we danced until we were both very tired. She was easy to talk to, and she made me feel like I was worth something. It was a special evening that led to many others just like it while I was in college. Martha and I dated through all four years of college. She was an exceptional person whose influence contributed to some of the best times of my life, times when I felt the most normal.

Because only a few females attended Texas A&M, the guys there nominated their girlfriends as sweethearts. To be voted an Aggie sweetheart was a big honor because only the prettiest girls were elected. Since I felt Martha was such a beauty, I nominated her. She won. Of course I'm biased, but I think she was the prettiest of all the girls voted in that year.

It intrigued me to be so attracted to someone with such a strong will. Martha knew how she wanted things to be, and nothing else would quite do. I considered her stubborn and even overbearing at times. But I was drawn to her. I couldn't wait until I could be with her again. My attraction to her was unusual because I was strong-willed and stubborn, too—there's something about being an Arterburn that carries with it the drive to do things a certain way, and no one else's way seems to matter. If I had followed a predictable path, I would have dated a girl who would allow me to believe that everything I did was okay, who would agree with me even when I was absolutely wrong. There were plenty of those around, but I fell in love with Martha. Some of our friends speculated that we might kill each other if we ever disagreed over something important. We were some couple to watch.

I believe that one of the reasons I liked Martha so much was that I thought she might protect me from what I sensed was looming just below the surface. Her strength gave me the security to feel that if my old problem cropped up, I would be able to conquer it with her help.

Even though I was so proud of her and proud to be her boyfriend, I doubt I ever told her that. I was too afraid to reveal just how I really felt. I don't know why, but I could hardly express an emotion back then. I never learned how. Maybe I thought my image would be ruined if I revealed a true emotion. I didn't want anyone to truly know who I was. I didn't want anyone to go below the rough and stern surface to find an uncertain and insecure little boy living there. It's sad to know I never took the time to put away my own self-interest to tell Martha what she deserved to hear.

I don't know if it was God's will for me to marry Martha, but I suspect that if I had it would have saved me from tremendous loads of misery. But if I had married her without first resolving my sexuality through counseling, I might have caused her even more misery. The qualities that drew me to Martha in the beginning, however, prevented me from making a commitment in the end. I wanted to be independent—not that I wouldn't settle down, but I wanted it to be solely my decision. I never wanted to be pressured into anything. I guess I was afraid that Martha would force me to marry her or at least pressure me to. So due to a combination of mixed emotions, I didn't allow our relationship to go beyond the dating stage. My fear of losing my independence prevented me from enjoying the satisfaction of starting a family and experiencing sex in the way God intended. Perhaps it was my respect for her or my fear of commitment, but during the four years I dated her, there was nothing physical between us. When I left college I left a clean vessel, a male virgin—as rare then as it is now. I believed that one of the worst sins a person could commit was sexual immorality, and I never succumbed to the temptation while I was in college.

I seriously dated only one other person during college—a beautiful blonde, also from Baylor. We met during one of the times Martha and I were parted due to some argument neither of us was willing to lose. This girl, also the daughter of someone in the ministry, lived in an exclusive section of Dallas. We dated some off and on, and I grew to care about her very much. But her father didn't want me to date her. He was a strong male, a minister of a Southern Baptist church, and his disapproval made me feel completely rejected. Maybe he wanted her to date someone with more money. Or maybe he wanted her to date someone from Baylor. Or maybe he recognized my sexual ambiguity. Whatever, his vision and desire for her certainly didn't include me. She dated me anyway, but I was unwilling to go on in the face of her father's summary indictment of my suitability. It hurt me, and I suppose it hurt her also. If there had been a second chance for me at marriage, it would have been with this young and beautiful Christian girl. But I broke up with her without giving any indication of how I felt or why I could not go on. I carried her father's disfavor with me for years, a disfavor that rekindled the feelings of alienation and rejection I experienced when I moved from Ranger to Bryan. Significantly, this rejection came from a man who was a minister, who supposedly represented the very character of Christ to others.

My college years were moral years but not years of spiritual growth. I rarely attended Sunday school or church. I was either at school studying or at some lake skiing. I loved to ski and had a fast ski boat that I owned with my younger brother Steve. I saw no harm in taking a break from my books and spending Sunday at the lake. I thought that since I had been in church almost every Sunday and Wednesday while growing up, I could miss frequently and still have attended more than most people ever would. But I didn't go to the lake to avoid worshiping God. I wasn't rebelling against church—at least I didn't think I was. In my mind, I was only getting some exercise and having some well-deserved fun in the process. But that wasn't all that was going on. Those fun times kept me out of church and out of an environment in which I could grow spiritually. I was experiencing the lull before the storm, and I was not preparing myself for the storm. There I sat through my college education acquiring all the knowledge I thought I needed while avoiding the most important need of all. I was stupid to neglect the spiritual part of my life. What a tremendous difference it would have made if I had acquired spiritual knowledge while the sexual temptations in my life were minimal.

I had been elected to the Student Senate and was made President of the Architecture fraternity. My grade point average was maintained at 3.75. I had sought recognition and honor and had received them. I learned to expect victory. I left college ready to take on the world, confident I would add to my victories. Instead, I headed out toward my defeat. I thought I was prepared for anything, but I wasn't prepared in the least for what was ahead. I was an intellectually gifted but spiritually retarded man who hadn't taken advantage of the strength and wisdom found in Scripture.

I had accepted a position with the Department of Housing and Urban Development (HUD) to work on a project for disaster relief. It took me away from home and on a journey into the real world, a world full of opportunity, growth, and achievement. That was what I wanted to do—grow and achieve—and have the opportunity to make some money. But the real world defeated me. In my efforts to conquer, I failed the test of living.

CHAPTER FOUR

The Making of a Career

The day after graduation I set out for my first assignment on my new job. I had signed on with President Nixon's Office of Emergency Preparedness. It was a division of Housing and Urban Development that functioned as a disaster assistance team. The first deployment of the team was to New Braunfels, Texas, to help with a tremendous flood back in 1972. It was our team's job to acquire housing for those who had lost homes in the flood. We were able to quickly set up communities of manufactured houses so people could move in within days of the disaster. That time it was a flood, but we were called on to help victims of tornadoes, hurricanes, earthquakes, and all the other "acts of God," as the insurance companies called them. It was an intense job. Everyone we dealt with was traumatized from losing all their possessions or even the rest of their family.

Following the New Braunfels flood, I met a man crying by the curb just outside a bar. His parents and their home had been swept away by a twenty-foot tidal wave from the flood waters. Authorities found his father dead downstream but couldn't locate his mother. He had searched all day for his mother without results. Finally, as he made his search through the golf course, he found her dead, hanging from a tree, her body about twenty feet off the ground. We cried with him and then went back to our rooms for rest.

About the time we were cleaning up our project in New Braunfels, some Indians up in Omak, Washington, were having some problems with snow that had melted a little sooner and in greater abundance than expected. An entire reservation was wiped out by the tons of water that came pouring down the hill. We helped the Indians get settled in some new quarters, and then we moved on to Pennsylvania to help some victims of the wrath of Hurricane Agnes. Twenty thousand people had been left without homes because of the high winds and rain. We arranged for shelter for all of them. There was something very special about those people in Pennsylvania. They were so appreciative of what we did there. We never left work at five o'clock; we stayed on into the early morning hours to help. But for some we could offer no help but to listen.

It was all very sad, traumatic and shocking, but I loved the work. The rewards of helping people were great. I was able to get out of myself and feel for others while I attempted to make a contribution to their lives. But I felt immune from the misfortunes those people experienced. I believed such tragedies could only happen to others, certainly not to me. I watched the drama of death and destruction and saw it as confirmation that my life was spared the hardships others had to endure. Who did I think I was? I was confused and had no idea just how nonimmune I was to life's adversities.

During my work with the Hurricane Agnes disaster, I met a woman named Carrie. The first night I was around her I knew she was someone worth knowing better. Her father was a political attaché to a European country. Needless to say, I was impressed. I could think of nothing more fun than flying overseas to meet the parents. But I didn't have to go that far. Their home was on the outskirts of Washington, D.C. When Carrie took me to her home, we drove up to a two-story, white, early Williamsburg home. I expected someone to walk out onto the porch in a velvet day coat and a white powdered wig. That beautiful place overwhelmed me and sparked a new fire of ambition in me. I wanted a place like that, and I wanted the woman that went with it. She was incredible.

Carrie was undoubtedly the happiest and most bubbly person I had ever met. She was seldom without a smile. No one knew how to have fun like she did. And she had such an infectious effect on those around her. It was most difficult to be in a bad mood with her around. She was sought after by many men, and I thought it was amazing that she liked me. She toured me all over the East. I was grateful to have someone like her show me Georgetown and Annapolis and all the other historical sites around the capital. It was as if she knew about everything and everybody. She made me believe I was important and that if I worked hard I could be a part of that world she knew so well. If I could have dreamed a new life for myself, it would have been with her, walking through Whaler's Village near Annapolis, seeing the sailboats in their berths and the little signs on the shops that looked like Thomas Jefferson had lettered them.

Several weeks later I took Carrie to Dallas, where my parents were visiting my aunt and uncle. I was pretty nervous about her meeting them because we had come from such differing backgrounds, but when she met them she was her usual bubbly self. She filled the house with laughter and excitement. I was really proud to have introduced such a prize. But my parents had a different view, and Mother didn't like her. She said that she was too hard looking, that she wasn't my type. Mother said Carrie was a little too worldly. After Mom put a damper on the relationship, I didn't pursue Carrie. I was living to please others and not making decisions that would be best for me, and it made me bitter. I was full of resentment. It would have been so easy for my parents to have accepted such a nice person with such an exciting personality. I'm sure Carrie went on to find that kind of acceptance, but it was a long time before I could forgive my parents for their rejection of her.

I finished my work in Pennsylvania and decided I wanted an assignment based in a more permanent location rather than just waiting for the next disaster in the land to occur. I wanted to have a place other than a hotel room to go home to after work. I talked to the regional administrator of Housing and Urban Development (HUD) about my desires. At the time HUD was giving out grants for renewal projects in towns all across America. There was one project in Easley, South Carolina, that interested me very much. The people in Easley had applied for a $1.3 million grant for a downtown renewal project. Essentially they wanted to take a group of stores that faced outward toward the street and turn the fronts to the back. That way, rather than looking out onto a street, the store fronts would face a common grassy area. The commons were to be made into an amphitheater with a clock tower. This would give the downtown area the feel of a mall and enable it to compete with the malls that had sprung up on the edge of town. I knew I could pull off the project. The regional director, whom I had become great friends with during the Hurricane Agnes flood, told the fine people of Easley that if they wanted the grant, they would need to hire me as executive director. They did.

I moved into that community and fit in from the first day. I loved the reception I received. I had come to save the town from drying up in the midst of new commerce being lured from the heart of the city. Other projects similar to this one had failed, but the people believed we could do it. I was a hero. The mayor, along with members of the Chamber of Commerce and various other civic groups in town, wined and dined me. I was invited to all the social events, and everywhere I went there was always someone who wanted a contract to work on the new project. My self-esteem had never been higher. But I had no one to show off to. When there is no one to share the feeling of "being somebody," it is almost a worthless experience. I needed someone to see what my life was all about. Two people came to see.

My younger brother had had a rough year at Baylor. He had become ill and was in the hospital for a while. Then the first day he returned to school, he had wrecked his car by running a stop sign. He was thinking about dropping out of school completely, and I encouraged him to hang in there and not give up. I suggested he spend the summer with me. He was so desperate that he accepted.

From the day he arrived, however, I think he set out to date every female in that town. He went nonstop, sometimes having two or three dates in one night. He was a wild man. It was good to have a family member with me, but it was troublesome from time to time. His late hours were irritating, and he was certainly not the best spiritual influence. But I was glad I could help him escape his problems. I believe that summer together allowed us to develop a bond that never weakened, even though we fought much of the time.

The other person who came to share my celebrity status was Martha. Since we had dated four years during college, I knew she was interested in me. I believe she came to Easley with a mission—a mission of getting me to marry her. But I wasn't interested in getting married. I was once more confused about who I was. All the fears and anxieties I buried during college grew up again. I wondered if I was normal or why I was not. There was no way I could make a lifetime commitment to someone. Knowing that Martha's intent was marriage and that I couldn't come through ravaged my emotions. When she left, our relationship was over. Martha had helped me control my sexuality. Now that she was gone, I had lost a real source of strength.

I became very involved in the Easley Baptist church. I usually attended before going out to the lake to ski. In fact, the habit became so natural that I agreed to teach a young boys' Sunday school class. I loved it. I loved the time I spent preparing the lessons. And I loved the reactions they had when they learned some truth or met some new biblical character. Teaching them helped me plug in spiritually. I was growing because the young boys caused me to grow. I took them on outings, to the show, camping, or whatever else I could think of. I was a good teacher, and the word spread around the church that I was doing a fine job with those young boys. When the preacher heard about it, he approached me with a request. He wanted me to preach to the entire church on Laymen's Sunday. I jumped at the chance. I told him I would love to, and I began preparing my sermon that night. I felt great about the prospect of standing in front of three hundred people and sharing God's truth. I believed it would be my finest hour.

While I was working on my sermon during the following two months, I was also getting to know some of the guys that lived in my apartment complex—four athletic young men who went to Clemson University a few miles away. It was great to have some guys my age to hang around with. They liked to drink beer and ski, and so we all did it together. They were nice looking guys, and there were always some cute girls hanging around their apartment. It was a fun place to be. Their company certainly alleviated any loneliness I was feeling. It was all innocent fun, similar to what I'd had with my friends from high school and college back in Texas. One of the guys seemed to like me considerably. He usually included me in what the rest were doing, or he would fix me up with a date from nearby Clemson University and we would go out together on a double date. I considered him my best friend that summer, and I liked being around him. He was full of wit and humor, and we played on the same softball team.

My times with him and the other guys were cut to a minimum as the time grew closer for my Laymen's Sunday sermon. From school I knew that preparation makes a big difference in performance, and so I prepared with great diligence. I was close to having the whole thing memorized by the time I gave it. It was exciting for me just to plan and pretend that I was in the pulpit giving the message. As the days came closer, the excitement grew and so did my relationship with God. I was going through questions of whether or not I should become a minister. I felt spiritually stronger than at any other time in my life. I felt I was on the verge of something great, and I was proud because I was doing it for God.

The evening of the Laymen's Sunday was a night to remember. The church was full of people. All parts of the service were conducted by church members. The man who sang the music had a warbly voice, but he put every ounce of enthusiasm he had into it. The whole proceeding led up to the moment when I was introduced to give the message. I nervously walked to the podium and began to address the congregation. It was the longest twenty-five minutes of my life. But I loved it. People there laughed when they were supposed to, and they even came close to crying in a couple of spots. I felt like nothing could compare with the sensation of doing something so significant as that. I was bumping heaven! Afterward the relief set in while the congregation came by and told me I had done a good job. They even made comments to the preacher that he had better watch out or I would replace him. It was a grand evening. One of the members said the nicest thing I ever heard. He said, "I'm glad I know you!"

*　　*　　*

What happened within the next few hours was in direct contrast with the experience I had at church, but in form it is similar to what happens to many others—ministers and laypeople—after a major spiritual victory. I believe many have been led astray in the hours following a wonderful experience with God. Our vulnerability to Satan is the strongest in the hours after a close and tiring walk with God. And I believe the reason so many of us are tripped up after victorious experiences is that Satan fights the hardest to destroy us during those times.

If we do nothing significant for the Lord, then we are not a threat to Satan and his intentions. Once we step out to achieve something of value for God's kingdom, Satan sees us as significant targets. I have talked to others who made one of the worst decisions of their lives right after a time of great spiritual accomplishment, and they share my belief in Satan's strategy. I reached a new low shortly after I soared the highest. Satan knew my weakness, and I succumbed to temptation. I have no one to blame but myself.

*   *   *

When church ended I drove back alone to the apartment. I was exhausted and drained of every ounce of energy. I should have headed straight for bed to rest and restore my strength, but I didn't. Instead I put on my bathing suit and went out to the swimming pool where some of my friends had gathered for a swim and some beer. I swam a little and then sat on the edge of the pool. Chuck, a local guy whom I didn't know that well, offered me a beer. At first I refused; it just didn't seem right to preach and then drink beer. But as we talked, I grew thirsty. The night was hot and humid, one of those South Carolina evenings that feel like the air is a warm blanket you can't pull off. So I had a beer and we talked for a long time. I don't know how much more beer I drank that evening, but I do know that I didn't stop with one or two. I was feeling a bit drunk by the time everyone left—everyone except Chuck. We laughed and talked and swam. Then we opened another beer and hung onto the end of the diving board while we talked into the night.

After midnight we were both tired, and since it was

a work day the following morning, we decided to go in. While we were still clinging to the diving board, Chuck told me what great fun it had been. He said he felt that we were more than just friends. I said I felt the same way. I was expecting to climb out and go home at that moment, but he surprised me by locking his legs around my waist as we hung by our arms from the diving board. I laughingly pushed him away, but I felt a familiar yet strange excitement. I definitely liked him more than as a friend. His touching me was all it took for me to tap into that feeling.

As I walked back to the apartment, I wondered what I was going to do. It had only been a short instant, but I knew what it would lead to. I knew the gates had been opened and the mounds upon mounds of emotions that had been pent up inside me for years were about to come out. I climbed the stairs to my bedroom and opened the curtains and stared out the window. I started to cry. I had a terrible feeling that I knew exactly what was going to happen, and I felt helpless to stop it. I went to sleep a very confused person.

The next morning I felt nothing but guilt. I was a miserable excuse for a person. At the point of greatest love for God, I had moved closer to the edge of a world I knew was wrong. I didn't know how God could or ever would forgive me. I decided that for as long as I remained in Easley, I wouldn't go around Chuck again—at least, I would never be alone with him. And I stuck to that commitment. But it hurt to carry it through. Here was the one guy who cared enough about me to express himself to me, and I rejected him. It was very difficult. But I managed not to weaken. I don't think he had any idea what he had done to me. I know he is unaware that he stirred up the emotions I had fought so valiantly to kill. From that night on, those emotions never ceased to haunt me.

My whole experience in Easley seemed to fall apart after that. Maybe, I thought, it was some type of punishment from God. The project I worked on had some budget overruns, and I was responsible. My desire for the town to have the best caused some expenses to run too high. I also failed to estimate how heat and humidity affected the speed of work in the summer. Some city officials became upset with me personally, and I had to resign. The real issue was that I had not awarded the contract to the right person. The problem was so bad that I feared for my life. I acquired a job back in Texas in the state planning division of the governor's office, and the former town hero spent his last night in town sleeping with a gun next to him. It was sad to leave that way. And when I left Easley for the city of Austin, all of my worst fears came true.

CHAPTER FIVE

The Door Blows Off the Closet

When I left Easley I hoped I would leave many of my problems behind, but I knew that I had not. The evening at the pool left its mark upon my emotions, and that, coupled with the way I left town, made me feel a sense of emptiness greater than ever before. I settled into my apartment in Austin and tried to ward off those unpleasant feelings by staying as busy as possible. I worked on personal projects and brought work home from the office. I couldn't allow myself to just sit and let my fears and doubts catch up with me.

To reassure myself that I was normal like everyone else and to maintain a steady flow of activity, I began to date regularly. Austin was full of beautiful women, and I think I must have dated most of them. I met quite a few women when I joined Hyde Park Baptist Church, a large church with a huge singles group. On a Sunday morning it was the "in" place to be. Doug was one of the most popular guys in the group. He was a real ladies' man, and women sought him out. I don't think he ever went one night without a date. As he and I became better friends, my dating life picked up considerably. Disco fever was just beginning, and Doug and I became a larger part of the scene in Austin.

To look at my behavior, one would have thought I was on the verge of finding the right woman and settling down. The dating frenzy appeared to resemble what so many others went through before they found a mate to marry. But for me it was nothing but a way to escape from who I was and how I felt.

*   *   *

I didn't realize it then, but I picked a poor method of coping with my problems. I should have sought out some type of professional help. I needed to talk about what I was experiencing. If I had just sat down with a counselor or a caring minister, I might have gone off on a different path. But instead I kept running, refusing to go through the pain of resolving the issues that were hurting me.

*   *   *

My church attendance grew more faithful than ever. I was drawn to that church and the people there. I accepted an invitation to teach a singles Sunday school class of forty or fifty young professionals just out of college. If I couldn't feel right on the inside, I at least wanted to do everything I could to look right on the outside. It was another wonderful experience. The need to prepare the lessons forced me to spend time studying the Bible.

I felt very close to God, and I experienced a deeper prayer life. I wanted God's will for my life, and I spent time on my knees asking Him to help me discover what that was. The more I prayed, the more able I was to pray honestly and ask God to help me with the real problem I faced—wanting to be close to someone of the same sex. I lusted after other men, and I wanted God to take that lust away from me.

In my prayers I took on the attitude of a victim, as if homosexual desires were done *to* me rather than *by* me. I asked God to intervene without my making any effort except expressing a wish. It was as if I thought I could continue living my life on the edge of destruction until God changed me. I walked close to the fire and expected God to turn down the heat. I didn't "flee temptation"—I got better acquainted. I went where the action was. I warmed myself in its company. I didn't "confess my sins"—I kept my problems a secret.

God didn't let me down by not answering my prayers. I let Him down by not doing what He told me to do in His Word. I expected God to do it all when just 10 percent of effort on my part would have produced dramatic changes. I *looked* great attending church and *felt* wonderfully spiritual teaching my class every Sunday. But that didn't matter because my heart was not pure in motive. Rather than working with God to help solve my problems, I left it all up to Him while I continued to let my problems grow. There were answers for me then, but I chose not to recognize them.

I mimicked Doug and his activity with the ladies. At least it kept me involved with a crowd of young people who were trying to live a good life. We had some great Christian friends, and I felt fortunate to be surrounded by so many quality people. My straight friends cared about me, but I had so many problems it was hard to accept their caring. We went on a skiing trip with some friends from Houston. We took a young girl from

Baylor who was struggling with anorexia. She weighed so little that I thought she would freeze to death up on that mountain in Ruidoso, New Mexico. We all worked together to help her, and it felt so good to be part of a group that cared for others. One of the guys on that trip went to the top of the mountain with me after everyone else had cleared the hill. He looked right at me and told me he loved our friendship. That meant so much to me, but I couldn't respond the way I wanted to. I wasn't used to telling people that I cared about them. But there they were, wonderful Christians who did care about me and wanted me to feel accepted.

*   *   *

Those wonderful straight friends are why I have such remorse about not opening up to anyone back then. I stress this again because no one can live successfully in isolation. A heart matures and finds its parameters as inner thoughts and feelings are shared with others. God never intended for us to have a one-dimensional relationship with Him. It must involve others. When it does not, a distorted reality evolves, a counterfeit of what life can become. Because I was unwilling to open up to anyone, I set myself up to fall totally away from everything I believed was right and good, even though I was surrounded by strong Christian men and women who could have helped me.

*   *   *

As my dating frenzy continued from the waters of Lake Austin to the night spots near the Capitol, I developed a restlessness that wouldn't go away. Even my

professional accomplishments weren't bringing any satisfaction. All I had was an impersonal list of what I had
done—and I had no one with whom to share the list. I
was beginning to realize that adding three or four more
items to my list of things done well wouldn't change my
void within. Nothing was gratifying about my dating
life. When the fun of dancing was replaced with uncomfortable moments of pretended intimacy, I felt cut off
from the real world that everyone else seemed to be
living and enjoying. I was even growing weary of the
independent lifestyle I had longed for during my college
years. Nothing produced satisfaction, but I didn't know
what was wrong. I was ready for something to happen,
and it wasn't long before it did.

I began dating a model, Lana, who worked for a
local agency in Austin. The Driscol Hotel had hired the
agency to do a brochure showing newlyweds enjoying
all the fine things of the hotel. Lana was asked to play
the part of the wife; I, the husband. Lana was bright and
very beautiful, and we liked each other from the beginning. It was fun spending the day working with her, and
so I asked her out after the photo shoot. We had dinner
at a nice restaurant in town and decided to find a place
to go dancing afterward. She told me about a place that
had just opened. She described it as "beautiful" and "exciting." According to her, it was an architect's dream, full
of art deco, neon lights, and modern sculptures. It
sounded like a place I'd really like, and I told her I would
love to go. Then she said there was one thing I needed to
be aware of—it was a gay bar, a "fun place." I had heard
about gay bars but had never been in one. She said there
would be a lot of straight couples there as well as gay
couples. Not really knowing what to expect, I agreed to
go with her.

When we entered, it was obvious that whoever had designed the place had tremendous taste. It was wonderful. Sculptures with green and pink neon were everywhere; bright lights circled the room. The music was the loudest and the clearest I had ever heard. From the minute I set foot inside, I was thrilled to be there. So much energy flowed through the place that it practically pulled us onto the dance floor. We danced and sweated and didn't stop for probably a full hour. I felt great. I had never been in a place that was so exhilarating. I felt euphoric and didn't want to stop dancing. As I danced and whirled, my eyes swept around the room registering faint images. As the night went on, those images became stronger and more distinct than the lights or the music or the neon sculptures.

The images were of young men standing around holding onto one another. One guy would have his hand in another guy's hip pocket, and another guy would be clutching the first guy's arm. They were close. It was apparent they cared about and accepted one another. Some of the guys were dancing together. There was nothing overtly sexual about anything they were doing. They looked like a bunch of close, male friends that were having a good time. It looked like all the men in the place—except me—were experiencing acceptance, caring, and love. Everything I longed for was being enjoyed by others as I watched. I had a strange feeling that I belonged there, that I needed to be with those guys. I felt comfortable and wanted never to leave. I had discovered a world I never knew existed, and yet it was the world I felt I was supposed to be in.

I didn't think about sex. I focused on the excitement and acceptance that were so prevalent. Couldn't I participate in all of it without having to be sexual? I was repulsed by that part of it; I just wanted to be part of something that could untie the knot in my stomach. It wasn't passion for another that attracted me; it was self-love. I wanted to satisfy my self, something I hadn't been able to do through my previous experiences. Somehow I thought I might find satisfaction in that place.

Call it a subconscious act of will, Freudian, or satanic, but for some reason I walked out of that place without my MasterCard I had used to buy drinks. When I reached for my card at lunch the next day, I realized what I had done. I knew immediately that I liked the idea of going back to the disco to retrieve it. After work I changed into some fresh clothes and made my way through the traffic toward the gay disco. My legs felt as if they were being pumped full of magnetic jelly. They had that feeling you get after you barely escape crashing your car. I was excited to return. I parked and went in and asked the man at the bar if he still had the card. He did, and he returned it to me after I showed him some identification. As I fumbled with it I was once again captured by the rhythm and the beat that came pounding from those speakers. I placed my card in my wallet and turned to walk out of the place. As I turned, there, standing right in front of me, was Randy, one of my best friends who was going to the University of Texas. I was stunned. Why was he there?

He had the same question for me. "Jerry Arterburn!" he yelled. "What the hell are you doing here in this place?" (I had no idea just how appropriate his question was. It was hell, disguised as the most exciting place on earth.) I was about to return the question to him, but before I could respond Randy grabbed my arm and took me into a back room I hadn't seen the night before. The room was filled with sofas where many male couples were engaged in private conversations. This guy was such a nice friend. I had no idea that he was gay. He had lots of friends and was a yell leader at the university. I couldn't believe it. I had seen him with girls many times, and I never suspected anything. He took me over to a table and asked me to watch one show with him. My telling him why I had come to the bar didn't seem to matter to him; he didn't care. He wanted me to stay and have a good time. We sat there and talked until the show started. When it did, a woman gowned in satin and sequins came out and sang. I thought she was terrible; my friend said that for a guy she wasn't bad.

Up to that point, Milton Berle was the only person I had ever seen impersonate a female—and he looked so stupid I thought no one else would want to. But I learned that's what a drag show is all about—dressing like and affecting mannerisms of women. What a strange way to be entertained. But it was more than entertainment. It was an introduction into a world I never knew existed, and it was the first of many new experiences I didn't initially understand. But Randy was going to take care of that. He was going to "bring me out." That's what gays call the process of transition from the straight world into the gay world. It means to "come out of the closet."

The process of my converting to a homosexual lifestyle didn't happen overnight. It was so gradual I didn't even know it was happening, because in the beginning I thought I was merely making new friends. I really enjoyed being around those new friends. They understood the way I had felt growing up. Eventually I began to envy their freedom of mind, their freedom of spirit, and their rebellious ability to go against the norm. I loved how everyone acted as if I was wonderful. It was the first time I felt truly accepted.

As I spent more time around homosexual men I became an experimenter. I thought that what I was doing was wrong, but I wanted to give the lifestyle a try. I wanted to know if the straight world had been all wrong about sexuality. I wanted to find out if this secret society had the answers for the way I felt. So I brought my dating frenzy to an abrupt stop and began spending all my spare time with a gay couple from Texas University. I meshed easily with them and their lifestyle, and they took me in like a brother. They gave me a feeling of closeness I never experienced with my own brothers. The feeling of being accepted was overwhelming. That acceptance, more than any other aspect of the gay world, hooked me into the culture.

*   *   *

I know that everyone hasn't had the same experience in the gay world, but many men would recount similar circumstances. At one of the most vulnerable times in my life, I walked into a homosexual trap, and I willingly stayed ensnared for seven years. That's why it is important to explain what seduction is all about. I was seduced by homosexuality, but there are many parallel seductions that attract the unwary—money, power, drugs, or extramarital heterosexuality. In fact, I relate my experience very closely to a drug. I took the "homosexual drug" for the same reason that others take chemical drugs: I wanted to feel better; I wanted to be accepted; and other things hadn't produced satisfaction. By taking that "drugged" route, I could avoid the pain from my past for a while. That's what seduction is all about. It's a promise to deliver what ultimately will break you. But at the time it makes the forbidden more appealing than anything else in the world. The appeal of that forbidden world unfolded in deeper levels of involvement.

*   *   *

At first it all looked like a bunch of fun people doing things and going places that everyone would want to do and go. They were not just fun people, either. They were young executives with good jobs and bright futures. They were athletes from every imaginable sport. And they were college kids, frat rats, that were always looking for something to do that would be exciting and a reason to have a party and bring people together. All these groups tugged at me to spend time with them. They wanted me to be part of the group, an accepted member of their crowd. Whenever they tugged, I agreed to go join the fun. I was rarely alone in my spare time. There was always someone wanting me to go somewhere or someone wanting to come over and spend time with me. It was very attractive to be in demand, but within two months of this kind of life I knew it was wrong in every way.

Frequent, unbidden fears lay beneath the surface of my new lifestyle. What if I were to have a heart attack right in the middle of ———? What would my family think when they heard how I died? What would Martha or Carrie think if they found out? What if God didn't understand what it was like to be me? Didn't God *know* how miserable my life had been? I found myself begging God to understand. My prayers became a confused jumble of pleading for forgiveness and of bargaining for His okay while I got it out of my system. The rationalizations I used on myself, I tried on God—and hoped fervently He knew I was sincere. I carried around the shifting weight of guilt. Maybe the church back home was wrong, maybe homosexuality isn't a sin . . . but maybe the church was right, then what would I do? I knew it would be difficult to get out. Like most drugs, homosexuality can be addictive. Once you taste it and feel its effect, it is very hard to give it up.

Because of my modest beginnings and my desire for more money, I was always attracted to money and those who had it. One of the fascinating aspects of the gay world is how much money is spent by gay men in an attempt to have a good time. Someone always had an acquaintance who wanted to spend big bucks on a lavish three- or four-day party. When I was in Austin, I found it hard to believe the number of wealthy kids, from the best of Texas society, that were gay. They would somehow grab onto some of their trust funds early and spend it on their friends. Planes were chartered so that everyone could fly to New Orleans for Mardi Gras, one of the largest gay celebrations in the world. (The New Orleans fly-ins were a time to meet other gays who would also fly in from all over the world to join the celebration there.) Boats were rented so that everyone could cruise the ocean for days at a time on one long party. Celebrities from sports or television or the movies would show up at these parties, and we never knew whom we might meet at the next marathon of merriment. These famous, powerful, and rich people made us all feel good about ourselves. If they were gay and they had it all, then we must be okay. Those of us who were caught up in them rarely examined the superficial nature of those values.

Because so much money was available, there was a corresponding abundance of drugs. Many of the guys had friends who were physicians that supplied them with uppers and downers. If there was a chemical anyone wanted, it was available somewhere for the asking. People would openly snort cocaine and at times freebase. Almost everyone drank and drank heavily. Drug addiction and alcoholism were black clouds hovering behind the laughter and loud talking. Sometimes a flicker of insight revealed the shallowness of purpose and character engendered by too many drugs or too much alcohol. But issues of that sort weren't discussed— they belied the illusion that the gay life was the good life. And when those issues did surface, or when the pangs of conscience began to hurt too much, more booze and more pills provided quick fixes and easy escapes.

The crowd I ran with came mainly from one fraternity at the university there in Austin. About ten of us became close friends and did things together most of the time. We appeared to be a happy-go-lucky crowd with little on our minds except how to have an even better time tomorrow. If something sounded fun, then we wanted to do it. We were so busy living like rebels and looking for excitement that we spent no time considering critical issues. Our lives were off-center and directionless. We never discussed eternal life—a concept that was foreign to my friends. Since the AIDS epidemic, many gay men have been forced to consider what's ahead. But at the time, death and dying were relegated to the far corners of our minds since we were so occupied with living and having good times.

*   *   *

I wasn't smart enough to see through the "glamour." The gay world never appeared cheap to me. There was always someone new with money or power to add validity to what we were doing. The men in high positions were what attracted me the most. Position was more important to me than money because of my ties to the governor's office. I loved power and position. The gay men in government and politics seemed to have high ideals; they certainly weren't fools. I fancied some perfectionistic ideal that they had their act together and I could be just like them. It was all so deceptive that I wasn't able to see the reality behind the facade.

In looking back it is so easy to recall glaringly clear images of loneliness and emptiness looming heavy against the backdrop of forced fun and business. I remember encountering a Methodist minister one night in a gay bar on Sixth Street in Austin. He went there for one purpose, companionship. We talked about his life, and I commented on how rewarding it must be to have hundreds of people to minister to. He told me it meant nothing to him. He said that in all his ministry he had been unable to quench the thirst for acceptance and the desire to sit quietly and feel right with the world. He explained that his misery had been a constant companion, interrupted by one-night encounters that failed to fill his void, yet dug it deeper and wider in increasingly more painful strokes. I didn't think of him much back then, but I do now. I think of him as a messenger from God sent to bring me back, one of many I met along the way. But I didn't heed the message. I instead wrote it off to an old man who had been hurt. I never considered that his hurt might have been self-inflicted from years of painfully wrong decisions and that later I might experience that same hurt in my own life.

In that strange world of homosexuality I found a mixture of different types of people. Each one, like me, has a story to tell. From my discussions with them, I was able to place most gay men into three categories.

The first group comprises those who from very early in life had effeminate characteristics. They were outcasts who didn't participate in sports and rarely became involved with extracurricular activities at school. They are often referred to as "wimps," "sissies," or "pansies." Those men will argue that they were born gay. They do not differentiate between having effeminate characteristics and having sex with someone of the same gender. They believe that their feminine traits predestine them to a life of homosexuality. Some go so far as to believe they are actually women trapped in men's bodies. I believe that those men do have a biological problem and that perhaps they are deficient in some hormone or have an overabundance of some other kind. But I equate them with a heterosexual with an extremely strong sex drive that was perhaps brought about by an excess in some hormone. The heterosexual with an overabundance of testosterone might be tempted more than most to want to sleep with someone he is not married to, but hormonal imbalance does not make it right. The same applies to the homosexual who could be identified with homosexual tendencies from early on in life. Those tendencies, even though present from birth or early adolescence, do not make right what is forbidden in Scripture. With professional help and time and patience those tendencies can be controlled and often completely resolved. Testimonials abound from those who have found victory in change. The Bible says so many things that provide insight into every problem of life. The following verse says to me that if you trust Christ there is nothing you cannot conquer. Nothing, including abnormal sexual urges. Philippians 4:13 says, "I can do all things through Christ who strengthens me."

The second group of homosexuals, and I place myself in this group, are those who spend most of their lives as heterosexuals or asexuals. They are drawn into the crowd by repeated invitations to events that sound like nothing but pure fun and excitement. To go river rafting, water skiing, or traveling on a weekend trip somewhere out of state was a common invitation always open to me. Through these different events, normal friendships develop with people who are nice looking and have a good sense of humor. They don't fit the limp-wristed stereotype seen in the movies. Many of these guys are educated, and some are Christians who, like myself, have fallen away from God's will. Often they despise being homosexual and will try to go straight on their own. Some maintain a bisexual lifestyle; some are married. They all appear so normal. Then once the acclimation process is over and the uncomfortable feelings are quieted, homosexual acts are introduced. That is when homosexuality seems "natural" and hooks its new converts.

I feel this is the saddest group, perhaps because I was part of it. It is sad that so many well-intentioned and clean-cut men can be drawn into this world. The homosexual world awakens at midnight and becomes a place to let off steam or find some people to talk to. The places and the people gradually lead to a completely different sexual orientation, and soon the neophytes believe their sexual preference has existed since birth. That lie is a major part of the entire lie that ruins the lives of so many wonderful people. No matter how a person is born, God can help that person deal with the problem. The problem can be overcome if somewhere along the way the person is able to rebuke the homosexual lifestyle and repent to God of the sin. If not, the sin of homosexuality drags the person into a decline of self-destruction brought about by the lustful desires of the heart that must be abandoned. (If this sounds like I am preaching, please forgive me. I am only trying to relay what I was told but did not heed.)

The third group comprises the hard-core, embarrassingly effeminate men often portrayed in the media. They like the smell of leather and the idea of being totally controlled by chains wrapped around their neck or legs. This third group is more perverted than the first two groups. They are further into the lifestyle and their defenses are stronger. They are fighters for the homosexual cause and will usually attack anything that threatens or questions their way of living. If there is a group that has been turned over to a reprobate mind, it is this one. They have no remorse over the life they live. The lust they feel is the most controlling force in their lives—all other elements revolve around the lust and desire to experience sex in any bizarre form that can be imagined.

This trashy and filthy element allowed me and the others in my group to justify our actions. In comparison, we weren't so obviously bad. Our sin was lessened in our minds because we had not hit the extreme of our sin. The craftsmanship of Satan is awesome when you look at how he is able to use the worst of our world to help us justify only being a "little" wrong—anything to keep us from reaching our potential is good enough for Satan. I always used that third group to prove to myself how normal I was.

The lure of homosexuality is power, glamour, and money, but it is not all beauty. The filth of the lifestyle is never more evident than in the bookstores that spring up on almost every corner in certain sections of big cities, where pornography of the worst kind is disseminated along with all types of sexual paraphernalia. Those are the places where gay men go when their loneliness is the greatest. There are thousands of pictures and images, both still and moving, of homosexual acts in thousands of forms. Behind the stacks of smut there are back rooms where couples can come together, perhaps after knowing each other for only a few minutes, and act out their fantasies or watch a movie of the sex acts being performed. In some cases live acts are performed for small audiences in those dark cubbyholes where the sickening stench of spent body fluids has saturated the walls.

Many men go to those places in search of satisfaction, and I have no idea how a civilized society can allow such places to exist. They reflect the worst of homosexuality and the horror of gay life, but they should not be used to judge those who are trapped inside that horror. As caring people, we should turn the intensity of our disgust into desire to help those who are trapped to escape. Many are trapped in that sick society who had no idea what they would become once they succumbed to that first temptation. We need to help make them aware that there is hope.

Before Austin, Texas, I didn't know of any world other than the one I had grown up in. But I discovered there a hidden world where a dark door in an alley could lead to an underground of bright lights and brilliant music. I found that hidden world to be so attractive that I was willing to put on the shelf all the things I held dear. I split my life down the middle and tried to exist as two people—one in a world where everyone is distant and unconnected, the other in a world where I felt wanted. I wanted to be part of that alternate world. To do so I had to pay a price, and that price increased greatly when the deception of homosexuality became apparent. I wanted out, but I found myself miserably trapped in a double life.

CHAPTER SIX

The Lie of the Double Life

I knew from the very beginning that what I was doing was wrong. There was never any doubt in my mind that this was not the way God intended for His children to live. I did not like the lifestyle that I was in. I never felt comfortable about being there after those initial experiences. Once the thrill was gone it was replaced with rationalizations and justification of my behavior. I knew deep down that it was a sin. I read in my Bible that it was a sin. But I refused to act based on that knowledge. The attraction of the homosexual world was more powerful than my desire to do what was right.

Instead of resisting the gay world, I clung to it for a new sense of meaning in my life. I did not know that everyone in the world hurt. I did not realize or would not accept the truth that pain is a part of life. I did not understand that to experience pain is to live. When I hurt, I thought it was because I didn't fit into the world as others did. I wanted relief from the pain, and I found that relief in the gay world. That world fascinated me. When I met other young professionals who were gay, I felt like I was in a special, secret club that few people even know exists—I certainly hadn't known about it for twenty-seven years. Whenever I went to gay bars in Austin and Houston, I felt immediately at home, and I turned against everything I was brought up to believe. Those places, with hundreds of fraternity brothers in crisp white and yellow and blue starched shirts, attracted men like me, who placed so much emphasis on looks and dress. When I walked in, I felt those lost souls were my friends; they cared about me, and I cared about them. That security, false and pretentious as it was, was hard to break away from or deny.

The feeling of togetherness was so important for me. It was almost as if the rules were reversed from the straight world. In the straight world, I found many games, much rejection, and the necessity for a lot of effort to find acceptance from the opposite sex. But in the gay world, it was as if we were all in it together. There was no battle of the sexes; there was acceptance and openness. Men didn't stand off and remain aloof. They were always ready to meet a new friend and develop a new relationship. I loved that feeling. I didn't experience it in any other way in any other part of my life. Such friendliness made it easy to develop a close camaraderie with others. I felt totally accepted by five others. (Of those five, two of them are now dead.)

One of the biggest deceptions that kept me in the gay world was the same philosophy that has infiltrated all of our society—the philosophy that if something feels good, or if something makes you feel better about yourself, then it must be good. The Southern Baptist environment I was raised in had left me with the exact opposite of that maxim. I grew up with the idea that those things that were fun and felt good had to be bad. That's not what Southern Baptists teach, but that's what I took from it. The gay world that opened up to me was in direct contrast. My gay friends functioned totally under the feel-good philosophy. They convinced me and themselves that we were born into this country to have fun all our lives, and being gay was just another way to do that. Feeling good was what it was all about. No rule was worth considering if it contradicted the basic rule that you had to discover and do those things in life that made you feel good. As a rebellious and confused Christian, I stayed in the homosexual world because of the pleasurable feelings I had when I was with all of those people who were set on having a great time.

One of the most uncomfortable aspects of the double life was the need to protect my image in the business world. I worked with some conventional men who might have fired me had they known of my other life. I went to great lengths to produce the image of eligible bachelor, but I guess my preference wasn't much of a secret to anyone. I was thirty-five and not married, and I usually was around another guy. I doubt anyone thought I was just slow to get married. But I continued to work at projecting my image as a "good ol' boy." Whenever there was a function at the Dominion Country Club, I would show up with someone so beautiful the other men would ogle in envy. There was a beautiful member of the board of directors of the country club that I really liked, and we spent much public time together. She was so enjoyable to be around that if I had any spare time I tried to spend it with her. Our times together were more important than the public image she helped me produce, but the more time we spent together, the better I felt about my image. I didn't want my professional colleagues to know what I was really like. I feared their rejection, and I couldn't afford it emotionally or financially.

The whole scheme of two identities was quite tiring. It was hard to keep everyone satisfied and almost impossible to keep track of who knew what secret. I developed a paranoia caused from years of wondering whether I would be found out. It took its toll on me emotionally and drained my spirits, but I was determined to keep up the facade. If I was out partying on a Saturday night, I made sure I was in church the next morning. And I always wondered whether anyone had seen me and whether anyone knew my secret. I longed to be just one person. The energy that it took to maintain my double life left me feeling empty and wanting a way out.

It makes no sense for a person to feel good and feel empty at the same time. Likewise, it makes no sense to love a lifestyle and yet hate it. But if gay men are always empty in their relationships and if there is total dissatisfaction, why don't they all eventually wander out of the homosexual world? They don't wander out; like myself, they stay there. There is a reason: alcohol and drugs. The good times feel good because alcohol and drugs fuel the delusion that it's all wonderful. Those chemical pleasures are part of the excitement, as well as the ointment that soothes a guilty conscience. I became dependent on alcohol, since I couldn't enter the drug scene like the others. I couldn't smoke marijuana because I was allergic to smoke; nor could I snort cocaine because I had sinus problems. So I had to depend on the more traditional alcohol, and I consumed gallons of it. It allowed me to continue my double life and prevented me from seeing the reality I had created for myself.

I was really two human beings, one with God and

the other apart from God. I had straight friends and gay friends. My straight friends in Houston were every bit the typical macho and manly men. We went out to eat frequently and traveled on snow and ski trips year round. We all admired each other. They knew nothing about my going to gay discos. Having straight friends kept me out of trouble because it allowed me to stay more on the surface of the gay world and not be dragged into its most decadent parts. I would go to church on Sunday mornings with my straight friends, and I even traveled with them behind the Iron Curtain to smuggle Bibles to a missionary. Those guys from Baylor were wonderful Christian men. They didn't bring me out of the gay world, but they kept within me the realization that God is alive and working in this world. They also inspired me with their faith.

That missionary trip was an experience I will never forget. Those were the good times. I cannot emphasize it enough that the events I remember as good were not the trips with other gay men; the good events involved the things I did that were pleasing to God. If I could have kept on the track of Christian friends and Christian service, I would have made it out of the gay world before it was too late. Instead, I alternated between the straight and gay worlds. It wasn't easy emotionally. I was too hooked on the gay lifestyle to be able to turn my back on it entirely, even though I did not receive the satisfaction from it that I had initially received. That satisfaction had faded away after my first few years as a homosexual.

It seemed strange that I could go on a weekend party with a group of gays and not enjoy it, yet I had no fulfillment from it. Deceit and jealousy abounded. Alcohol was necessary to obscure the truth of what was really going on around me. I wanted out. I wanted no part of it, yet Satan's power kept me bound to that world of lost expectations. I believe the lost expectations are why so many of us stay long after we have proven the answer is not to be found in the ways of homosexuality. I abandoned what was right because I felt justified in being different. I didn't set out just to live a gay life; I set out to prove that the gay life is good and wonderful. When it turned out to be anything but good and wonderful, I went back, intent on trying harder and harder so that eventually I could make it work. I sought self-justification. But it didn't work; the emptiness remained. No matter how much I hate to say it or admit it, I made a major mistake. I made some poor decisions and kept making them for a long time. And I repeated my mistakes over and over, hoping that eventually the right feelings would click in and I would be justified for my actions. So many, like myself, stay in the homosexual world rather than say they made a mess of their lives and must get free from it.

After three years in the homosexual world, I was able to get out. I became fed up with the way my life had progressed. I was ashamed and knew that I needed to change. I left those friends behind and went an entire year without any involvement in the gay world. But I tried to make the change alone. I obtained no help from a pastor or a counselor. I was so determined to handle everything myself. That decision to do it on my own was one of many that cost me my life. My ego got in the way of my survival. It is so hard to break completely from a world where there is so much acceptance and open affection. I can only imagine how hard it is for those who have been involved for almost their whole lives. For me it was impossible to get out on my own and stay out. It was only a year later that I found myself back where I had been before. The Scripture 2 Peter 2:22 held true in my case: "But it has happened to them according to the true proverbs: 'A dog returns to his own vomit,' and, 'a sow, having washed, to her wallowing in the mire.'"

My guilt was intense when I slipped back into the homosexual world. I couldn't rationalize that what I was doing was right in any sense, but I was out of control. Like the adulterer tormented with guilt, I would return to sin for relief from guilt. Each incident increased the guilt and the agony of my double life. If those few who were aware of my attempt at change knew I had gone back to my old ways, they would be disappointed. And I didn't even want to think about the way God viewed me. I feared I was a total outcast from God's kingdom and there would be no way for me to return to a life in His will. I feared I had crossed the line from which none retreats and my sin would be unforgiven. I attempted to drive out those thoughts through alcohol, and a return to sin. It was not too late to repent and turn back, but I was still trying to justify my behavior rather than adjust it to God's plan.

Those looming questions of *why* must be answered: Why would a Christian become involved? Why would a Christian *stay* involved? There are no easy answers. But from another perspective, there is one simple answer—sin. The pleasure of sin anchored me to the gay life. Why do so many heterosexuals commit adultery? Sin.

Sin, for a while, is exciting and fun. It allows us to tap into the dark side of ourselves and rebel with full force. The power of sin is such that it can pull any Christian into any sin. Add environmental influences (such as early homosexual experiences) to the power of sin, and a perfect trap is set for a lonely young man starved for male affection and acceptance. So I solved my problems through the ways of the world and not the ways of God. If I had been a teenager that liked to read the Bible, things might have, or at least could have, been different. But when I needed to take the Scriptures and their truths seriously, I was unwilling. God's inviolable laws were violated regularly by me. The guilt that came from those violations pushed me to further justify what I was doing.

A real Christian can get caught up in homosexuality the same way that ministers can get caught up in extramarital affairs. In fact, I would not be surprised if those preachers who yell the loudest about homosexuality and show the least love for homosexuals are marred by some personal infidelity they are covering up with their campaign against homosexuals. Some would argue this point, but the sin of homosexuality is no worse than other sins. Those who elevate it to a greater sin may do so to justify their own lives outside of God's will.

I knew that God hated homosexuality, but I also knew that He loved me and all the other homosexuals. I knew there was forgiveness for all of us. That God is always waiting, ready to pick us up and dust us off, is the miracle that made the most difference in my life. He hated my sins of homosexuality, but He loved me, and He loves other homosexuals, too. All those thoughts rattling around in my mind, thoughts in direct opposition with my actions, made me a double-minded, confused young man. I had the knowledge of right and wrong, and I defied it. Those things made my predicament of the double life more painful and more incohesive.

Although I was never completely immersed in the homosexual lifestyle, I was a homosexual in the same way that a person who commits adultery is an adulterer. Once the adulterer quits having sex outside of marriage, he or she is no longer an adulterer. In that sense, I could be classified as a homosexual when I was involved sexually, and that wasn't often. The double life I led kept me on the fringes of the homosexual world.

It's really not that important for me to clarify or to know intellectually the intensity of my homosexuality. The important thing to me is that I am not a homosexual now. I profess that homosexuality is a sin. It is not the way that God intended for us to live on this earth. Nothing good can come out of it. What does come from it is total destruction of mind, body, spirit, and the ability to utilize God-given talents to accomplish great things for His glory.

Many factors worked together to keep me in the homosexual world. One strong factor had to be Satan and his tight grip on my life. I was not my own at that time in my life. There were resources available to help me, but I didn't use them. I tried to deal with it alone and I lost the battle. Whether I was possessed by demons or whether I was simply controlled by the devil, I don't know which. But I do know it was one of those two options. Satan took my opportunity and destroyed it. The one thing that I wanted to do was to serve God and minister to His people. And while I was headed that way, Satan turned me toward another destination.

When I was very young I sold Bibles door to door. One of my best summers was spent working at a Baptist encampment in New Mexico called Glorieta. I taught Sunday school all through my life. And one of the greatest moments of my life was when I preached at the First Baptist Church in Easley, South Carolina, to kick off their youth week. Those memories are meaningful to me. Those times represent what God wanted for my life. But Satan used homosexuality to rob me of my potential, and it is robbing others who are now living in its clutches.

From the first night I walked into that disco with Lana, I knew better than to become involved with the homosexual crowd. But I succumbed to the temptations of camaraderie, acceptance, money, power, and all of the other thrills. I bought a bill of goods from some well-meaning people who had no idea that homosexuality brings defeat, tragedy or even death. My friends thought they were doing me a favor by uncovering within me what they thought had to be released. And I was miserable enough at the time to grasp for what they were offering. Once in, I tried unsuccessfully to get out on my own. But I was unwilling to go through the pain of making that choice until it was too late. I never fully knew the great promise that could come from change. I would change, but it would be amid heartache and sorrow for my whole family and myself.

CHAPTER SEVEN

Telling My Parents

I moved to San Antonio and accepted a job with a group of developers who were building an elite country club, the Dominion, on the edge of San Antonio. I was in charge of the project and responsible for ensuring that the construction was of the finest quality and that we stayed on schedule. It was a wonderful job working with some fantastic people. We created a paradise on earth with almost every comfort imaginable. We brought craftsmen in from all over the world to work on that complex. It was all done before the collapse in oil prices hit Texas, and so we had no problem in finding buyers for the homes we built. The Dominion is one of those places that must be seen to be believed and understood. Through the building phase we were daily making changes and creating new things that had never been done before. It was an exciting job, and I put in at least eighty hours a week on it. I believed it would be a stepping stone to even greater opportunities as my reputation for quality became known.

But it was not to be. My double life as a Christian and a practicing homosexual had become too much for me to bear. I could no longer tolerate believing one set of values and living another. I didn't feel hypocritical, I felt fraudulent. All my life I had been results oriented, and I finally began to look at the results of my life. All I had accomplished was blotted out because of my homosexuality. Meaning and fulfillment had completely escaped me. I was left empty. Once again I determined I would leave the gay world and develop a normal lifestyle. I wanted no more of the jealousy and bitterness I could see so clearly in the lives of my homosexual friends. I had had enough of the misery. My conscience screamed at me to change, and I had no choice but to listen.

I explained how I felt to Tony, my roommate of six months, and he tried to see our relationship from my perspective. He didn't agree with my decision, but he respected it. He planned to stay at the house only until he found other accommodations, and in the meantime we led separate lives.

It was not easy getting out of the gay world. There were some great friends that I had to say good-bye to. There were others I just never saw again. And I was more lonely than at any other point in my entire life. The excitement and the action so prevalent in the gay world were replaced with the quieter activity of sitting in front of a television, alone. I began to read the Bible again to try to hear what it really said. I had heard so much rationalization that I had come to consider the Bible an opinion on life and not an ultimate authority for living a fulfilling life. I was able to allow the truth to sink in and confirm there could never be joy for me in the homosexual world. I started to go to church more often than ever before. I felt that God used each sermon to help me see a new truth about Him and my life as a

Christian, and this helped me in my transition. My work also helped. I stayed busy and poured myself into every detail of the construction of the Dominion. With new confidence, I was determined that I would no longer live the life of a homosexual. So far as I was concerned, I was completely out.

I guess I expected those days of struggle to be the beginning of a new life of victory after victory. I thought my commitment to change would be my first step toward a new life of joy and happiness. But there was one major problem I hadn't expected: AIDS.

* * *

In April of 1985 I came down with pneumonia, which so weakened me I had to be hospitalized. I had felt some growing fatigue, but figured the prolonged hours of work were finally catching up with me. I entered the hospital knowing that I had a severe case of pneumonia but also I would recover from it. I actually welcomed the hospitalization because I needed to take some time off work and rest.

For three days, tests and more tests were run on me. I was beginning to get suspicious that something might be more seriously wrong with me than I had expected. My doctor ordered numerous blood samples to check and reverify some of the tests. The remote possibility that I might have AIDS didn't occur to me until one day when the nurses started wearing rubber gloves and gauze masks. When I asked about the extra garb, I was told that the doctor had determined I was infectious and he would talk to me about it that evening. I felt like a leper. No one would touch me, and their looks seemed to cut through me.

The handwriting was on the wall: There is a major plague in the land, and Jerry Arterburn will not escape it.

The months that followed my diagnosis and discharge from the hospital were very depressing. So little was known about AIDS in 1985, and the size of the outbreak was just then coming into focus. But I knew from the number of my friends who had died that it was a serious killer. I felt that Americans probably thought of homosexuals as sleazy and disreputable, yet I knew it was only a matter of time before doctors, lawyers, movie stars, and persons from all walks of life would begin to come down with the disease.

Since I really was not ill after recovering from pneumocystis pneumonia, I continued to work for another year and a half. None of my colleagues knew of my problem as I continued my job as Executive Vice President of the Dominion Group, Limited. It was tough. I went to great lengths to ensure no one knew I was sick. I went home for lunch, not to eat but to sleep, so I could make it through the afternoon. Some days I didn't make it through the afternoon. I would be so exhausted by 2 P.M. I could barely drive myself home. I would walk in the house, lie down, and not wake until my alarm went off the next morning. I had no energy for a social life or even for a few friends. I just struggled to stay employed and to stay alive.

I didn't have any manifestation of AIDS other than the complete exhaustion I felt every day. I drew closer to God than ever before, and I studied my Bible whenever I could. I felt I was on a crash course toward spiritual growth. No major changes occurred during that time, and I was almost able to completely deny I had the disease.

Other than the fatigue, I felt just like I had always felt. I didn't "feel" like I was living with a killer disease, and that enabled me to delay having to reckon with the reality before me. I constantly stared in the mirror to determine if it was noticeable that I had AIDS. I compared what I saw in the mirror to the picture I had of myself. Every grey hair and every wrinkle and every bone that pressed against my skin caused some alarm. My weight loss was one thing I couldn't hide—I was thin to begin with, and my disease made me look thinner.

I faced my certain future alone. I didn't tell my family about my diagnosis. My reluctance to talk about AIDS was part shame and part unconscious belief that it might magically go away—or at least that it might not get any worse.

* * *

The casket was open at the front of the little church in Ranger, Texas. It was a sad but sunny day in the fall of 1985. The church was loaded with family and friends who had come to pay their last respects. Flowers covered the entire front of the church. People walked by the coffin and commented on how natural the body looked. Women in hats wiped their tears as my older brother Terry read the eulogy. After the service the procession moved slowly from the church to the top of Ranger Hill where other townsfolk had been buried, one just that morning. The crisp west Texas wind blew up the red sand into the mourners' faces as the preacher uttered the last words about my grandfather that no one would remember. Dad Art's strong will could take him no further. Just off the dusty road some little blue flowers fought the wind to maintain their beauty. People either fought back tears or wiped tears away. It was one of the most difficult days of my life.

I wondered if the cemetery where they would put me would have flowers as pretty as those little blue ones. Would those in attendance remember me for how I died or how I lived? I wondered how many people would show up, or whether most would forsake the entire occasion because of my illness. I hoped that my casket would be as nice as my grandfather's. As I had looked at him lying there with the casket open, I had not seen his face but my own. I had seen my own face as it would lay exposed in an open coffin six months, a year, or maybe even two years later. I had no idea how long I had to live, but I had accepted the reality. Barring some miracle, I soon would die.

I had stood with my cousins who had the duty of carrying my grandfather from the church. I was not able to help them because I was too weak. I was still without strength from my bout with pneumonia six months earlier. I didn't think anyone suspected there was anything wrong with me. But on that day I had to allow for a small leak in my cover-up. I told my brother Steve I couldn't carry the heavy casket of my grandfather. He looked at me as if he knew exactly why I was still weak from a six-month-old problem. (Later that day he asked me face to face if I had AIDS; of course I denied it.)

I knew that there would be other things that would lead people to conclude I was not well. And I knew that it wouldn't be long before the AIDS virus would devastate my body and destroy my appearance of health. Sooner or later I would be faced with revealing the truth about my condition. And, of course, then everyone would know I had been involved with homosexuality.

As the gravel crunched under the tires rolling away

from my grandfather's new grave, shame and remorse enveloped me, and I began to cry behind my dark glasses. I faced the grim reality of revealing my darkest secret.

I did not tell my mother or father until a year after Dad Art's funeral, a year and a half after my diagnosis. I wanted to spare them from knowing that their son had AIDS until I had no other choice but to tell them. A year and a half after my first bout with pneumonia, brought on by my deficient immune system, I came down with it again. I appeared to have a very severe infection and woke up one morning with a fever of 104°. My bed was saturated with water. There was a pounding in my head like I had never felt in my life. When I called my doctor he said to go directly to the emergency room.

My preparations to leave for the hospital became quite a struggle. While I was getting ready I decided that maybe I should not go at all. Because of the delirious state induced by the fever, it took me about three hours to bathe and arrange things so I could leave. I feared that I might not return, that I was going to die for sure. I decided it might be better to commit suicide than to die from AIDS and have my parents ridiculed and rejected because of my disease. I planned to kill myself rather than drive to the hospital. Since my parents had no idea what was wrong, they would never need to know that AIDS had killed me. I thought that having another suicide in the family would be less cruel than the knowledge of death from AIDS. I developed my plan fully, which included dying while I read my Bible and listened to a tape of Christian music by Steve Greene. But in the middle of my plan, something would not let me do it. I aborted the plan and resumed my preparations to leave.

Since I was not going to commit suicide, I realized

the need to tell my parents. It was time I got my personal things in order. I needed to develop a will. I needed to dispose of my personal property, sell my car, sell my house, and move out the furniture. Things had to become organized so people would know where to find them. All these details raced through my feverish brain. I had put off all those last acts, and now they all flashed in front of me. I was dying, and I had to prepare to die. I needed my parents to help me. I hoped that when I told them they could handle it. I thought they would be able to. I was a bit afraid that they might reject me like the families of so many others had done. It was scary to think they might turn away from me when I needed their help so badly. But even with the chance they might reject me, I had come to the time when I wanted them to know. They had a right to know. I had a responsibility to give them the chance to respond in a loving way. It would be wrong for me to keep it from them any longer.

Before I left for the hospital, I stopped to pray. I told God that somehow I needed Him to show me that He was still with me. Those Old Testament Scriptures where God turns His face away from those who continued to sin bothered me. I worried that maybe my illness was a judgment, and I asked God to show me a sign. I trusted that He would come through. Finally, on that cold, gray winter morning, I wandered in my car through the streets of San Antonio to find the hospital. That I even made it there should have been miracle enough. Almost unconscious, I stumbled into the emergency room and collapsed. They rushed me into a bed in the back.

At the hospital I underwent a battery of tests that determined I was suffering from some type of infection. *Infection* is a deadly word for someone with AIDS to hear—and I knew the chance for death within the next few hours or days was very real. I was in bad shape, and the medical staff wouldn't even let me call my parents. They wouldn't even let me contact them after I'd been moved into the recovery room. So I turned over on my side and tried to sleep. At that point I felt nothing was left. I thought of how I had made a complete mess of my life. I thought of the incredible opportunities God had given to me, some I had taken advantage of and many I had not. I asked myself, *Is this it? Is this the very day life will end for me?*

The infection that invaded my body was superior to my defenses, and my immune system was knuckling under to microscopic enemies. I felt utterly defeated, incapable of resisting further assault. The sheer effort to stay alive demanded more strength than I could muster. A deep, disturbing anxiety churned in the pit of my stomach; a nameless terror lodged in my throat. Remorse and helplessness overwhelmed me. Was God still with me? I began to pray earnestly. *God, if You are here with me, please let me know. I can't go on alone. It's all in Your hands. Please, God, if You just acknowledge that You are here with me, I'll live my days for You.* I let go of any pretense that I had the power to do anything about my life.

What happened next was a miracle. There came over me an incredible, comforting peace. It seemed like I was bathed in warmth and goodness that reached my very soul. I no longer felt anxious, I felt assured. The terror I had experienced was gone—joy had taken its place. And even though I yet suffered the physical ravages of illness, I felt spiritually strong. The suddenness of my emotional turnaround was startling, but fast on the heels of my bewilderment was the realization of what had occurred. God had answered my prayer. He was giving me a sign. He had not abandoned me! I knew I had nothing to fear.

When they took me to my room I was gleeful. Nobody could understand why I was so happy and at peace. I knew I had a deadly infection, but I wasn't crying or moaning. I had no earthly reason to be happy. My blood count was horrible. One nurse told me they had done all that they could for me, but even that didn't affect my spirit. I didn't let it. I thanked her and told her that what they had done was quite enough. I was happy to know that God was still on my side.

Even though I had become a Christian long ago, it was in that emergency room that I finally left the driver's seat of my life. I told God that He had my body, mind, and soul. I was done and I was played out. I asked Him to take over. Then the comforting power of the Holy Spirit flooded my life and allowed me to feel the warmth of being in the total care of Christ. I had been missing that most fantastic feeling all my life, but I was granted the opportunity to know it. What a tremendous gift of God's grace!

Visitors who came to see me in the days that followed listened to me as I shared with them how powerful Jesus is and how He had given me His strength so I could live longer. I told them He had reached down at what was my lowest moment in my life to renew my spirit. He set my heart and mind back on His promises, neither to leave me nor to forsake me. In my pain and torment, I had experienced a revival. In a miraculous way I had been touched by God. It was my turning point.

That night the nurses called my parents, told them of my hospitalization, and suggested they come the following morning. When my parents showed up they were alone. They walked to my bed with their shining faces glowing. They couldn't have hidden their expressions of love for me even if they tried. We hugged each other, and all of us began to cry. Then I looked my mother in the eye and said what I believe she already had concluded. "Mother, you have a very sick boy on your hands. I never wanted to have to tell you this, but I can't go another day without your knowing what I am experiencing. I am sorry to have to put you through this. I have the virus. I have AIDS."

From the first moment they heard that devastating news, they supported me. They hugged me and told me that nothing I had ever done or would do would prevent them from loving me. They said they wanted to help me. They said they would hang in there with me and back me all the way. They wanted us to be a team. Then they mentioned the most important thing I needed to hear: they asked me to go home with them. Unless one has been in that situation, it's difficult to imagine what that meant to me. My parents weren't ashamed to take me back. I knew they loved me, but the intensity of their ability to care about me overwhelmed me. Those two Christians, both incredible witnesses for God, set out to support their homosexual son in every way possible. It was incredible to experience that kind of love and acceptance. In spite of the hurt they felt, in spite of the ramifications that news of AIDS would engender in a small Texas town, they did what God did—they loved me anyway. They reacted in direct opposition to the way the world reacts.

When I awoke the next day, I realized I had some decisions to make. I had to decide how I was going to live the last months of my life. In 1985 the prognosis was for a person to live about six months after the first case of pneumonia, and I had already lived a year and a half past my first bout. It was hard to face, but I had to make every day count from then on. I was determined to do it. I knew I had to get my act together quickly, and so I began to dig into the Word of God. For the second time, I reached back in my memory for the verse from childhood that would become my battle cry—Philippians 4:13, "I can do all things through Christ who strengthens me."

I had received my sign from God that He was with me. Now, with the help of Christ, I was going to persevere. I was going to say no to my doubts about God and His love and I was going to say yes to His love and my faith. I refused to listen to those who would have me believe that what I was experiencing was a form of punishment from God. I refused to accept the concept that what had happened was the judgment of God. I knew God wasn't "getting back at me" because I was a homosexual. My getting AIDS is not an act of cruelty on the part of God. The destruction of my physical body may be complete, but my soul is reserved for heaven.

CHAPTER EIGHT

Living with a Killer Called AIDS

With each new revelation that I was not improving, I dug deeper for more faith in God to see me through. I knew He would provide whatever I needed to make it through all of the pain. (I only wished that in the process He would leave a little more hair in place.) I was optimistic about my future. I knew most people died from AIDS, and I figured I would die, too. But until that time I decided to live with it—I don't mean exist or survive, I mean *live*. I wanted to take whatever time I had and make it the most valuable of my entire life. AIDS had my body, yet I knew faith would protect my soul and attitude could preserve my mind. So I fought back my doubts and fears in order to use whatever time I had left for living. I said to myself, "Let the celebration begin."

The place I could do the most good was at the hospital bedsides of those who were in the last stages of AIDS. I promised God that I would spend time with those with AIDS who were alone, and especially those who were without family and friends. I wanted to minister to them in person while I was living, and I hope that once I am gone, this book and my videotape will continue to help those who need to know the reality and the power of Jesus Christ in their lives.

As it turned out, one of the most difficult tasks was returning to the hospital for treatment. The people on the staff were caring and tried to make the visits as easy as possible, and their love and concern motivated me to love more and care more for others. But it was difficult to overcome the sadness that swept over me upon seeing the other patients whose disease continued to drain the life out of them. Each visit brought back the reality of just how terrible AIDS is and how much damage it does to its victims. Persons, who months earlier were pictures of health, would be in wheelchairs, too weak to walk. Emaciated faces revealed weight drops below ninety or even eighty pounds. Seeing their conditions eradicated any remnant of denial that the disease is a deadly killer. Those were tough visits.

Physical evidence was only part of the trauma I witnessed. Some of the worst scenes were created from those who showed no evidence of the disease's destruction. Married couples came in who looked like typical yuppies, young professionals who "had it all" very early in life. But the strain on their faces revealed the underlying terror they were experiencing. During the visit they would be informed that one or both of them had the AIDS virus. Often it was because of one's unfaithfulness in marriage. Occasionally it was due to one's contracting the disease before marriage. Their visit would consist of many tears, sometimes screams of anger, and at times violence, as one lashed out at the other because of the infidelity.

There were also the sad cases of children who had contracted the virus from transfusions or from mothers who had the disease when the children were born. Those kids didn't fully know what they had, but they were told they would not recover. They were real troupers, and their attitudes went a long way to brighten the hearts of each of us. No one ever called them "innocent victims" of AIDS. At least not there at the hospital. That would have implied the rest of us were "guilty victims," deserving of the fate we faced. None of us set out to have this happen to us. This was not caused by our own intentions. And everyone at the center treated us and the children alike. We were none of us "victims." We were conquerors over our fears and conquerors over a merciless plague.

On my visits back to the hospital I took the time to go by the rooms of those who were sick enough to be hospitalized and often in the last days of their lives. On one visit I had had a very rough day. My blood count had gone quite low, and I was greatly discouraged. But I was determined to go by and visit some of the patients on the third floor before I left. The third floor is where the more critical patients are cared for. It scared me to make the trip up the elevator because I didn't want to face the scene that would one day be my own. I went up and down the elevator four or five times before I garnered enough courage to step off the elevator. I wasn't going to turn back on the promise I had made to God in the emergency room. I told Him then I would go and witness to those who were ill if He would give me the opportunity, and I was determined to fight my fears and keep that vow. I went to the nurses' station and asked the nurse if there were some patients who needed a visitor. I wanted to know if anyone could use a friendly hello or if anyone hadn't had a visitor in some time.

The nurse told me of three men that hadn't had visitors for five weeks. For five weeks they had lain in their beds, often in tears, waiting for someone to reach out to them, but no one had come. Their families had turned their backs on them. I asked the nurse to point me toward the door so I could go in and do nothing more than be a friend. She told me of a young man down the hall and pointed me toward his room. I stopped by the drink machine to buy him some grape Hi-C, which she had told me was his favorite. When I walked in I saw that he was asleep. He lay there on his side and looked like a normal young man. I stopped there and stared at him. I thought, *What a shame this is, the destruction. What a horrible thing. And how unnecessary. The suffering is so needless. Why must Satan have his day?* I let him sleep as I left to visit the patient next door.

The next man I visited was in the worst shape of anyone that I had yet seen. His arms and legs were no larger around than quarters. He lay there on his back with his bony knees brought up to his chest in a fetal position. He didn't have a hair on his head; it had all fallen out from the therapy. He was a prisoner of the disease, and he looked as if he had just been released from a cruel prisoner-of-war camp. He was shocked that anyone had come in, especially a stranger like me. He asked me in a soft but startled voice, "Who are you?" I told him I was Jerry and asked him who he was. He told me his name was Ron. I told him that I was an AIDS patient who was being treated on an outpatient basis and that I had stopped in to say hi. He broke into tears as he told me that it had been about five weeks since anyone had come to see him. His loneliness and isolation caused me to cry. He was part of a deserted group of people who are being treated like the lepers described in the Bible. I wondered, *Where are the local churches?*

*Why aren't they coming to minister to these people? As
churches battle for who is the biggest, couldn't they try to
be the most caring? When I am here, will no one come to
my side to encourage me?*

I left the hospital that day, as I did many others,
with a depression that nagged me to give up and give in
to self-pity. But I was determined not to do it. I wanted to
help those people, and God had given me the opportunity to do it. I would keep on doing it until I could do it
no more. But what I had seen made me want to make
my hospital visits as a patient as few and far between as
possible. It motivated me to stay as alive as possible so
that I would not have to face the death that lay in the
beds of that institution.

My job grew more difficult each day, and the strong
medication I took to fight off infection didn't make it any
easier. I wanted out of work, but I couldn't leave. I
wanted to travel and experience the freedom I had
never felt before. But I didn't quit for two reasons. One
was that I believed the busier I stayed, the healthier I
would remain. Although it was a struggle to work, I felt
that the struggle helped me with my will to live and the
strength I needed to survive. The other reason was
more practical. I needed the hospitalization insurance
that was offered with the job. Without it I would be
broke like so many of the guys I saw in the hospital.
Financially, the greatest asset I had was my name on
that policy.

From the time I contracted AIDS, I became isolated
and alone; I didn't have anyone to confide in. From the
start of my illness, I didn't have anyone to help me work
through my decisions. As a result, I made some big mistakes. One of them was to buy a new house; another
was to fill the new house with new furniture. I had

always wanted to have an estate home and a sports car (yet another big mistake). Such excellent examples of the foolishness of material possessions! I later sold them all at a major loss so my family wouldn't have to pay off any debts I had incurred. And what could be used by my brothers and nephews and nieces I wanted to go to them. I had no intention of their having a big garage sale after I died. All the buying and selling and giving away were confirmations of the finality of my circumstances. That I faced them alone made them much more intense than they had to be.

In October 1986 I contracted my first AIDS-related illness other than pneumonia—esophageal ulcers. My esophagus was covered with wrenchingly painful ulcers that made each swallow agony. I could tolerate only liquids or very smooth foods like Jell-O. I feared that one of the ulcers would rupture and I would bleed to death or that I would pass out from the pain and never wake again. Within two months I weighed less than a hundred and twenty pounds. The ulcers went away just before it became necessary to feed me through a tube in my stomach. It was hard not to spend hours wondering and worrying what the next strange illness would be and when it would strike. *Would the next illness be the one I wouldn't overcome?*

The illnesses and fears weren't the only weights I carried. I also had to cope with the emotional traumas I experienced each time another friend died. Each new death was as difficult to handle as the ones preceding it. We all shared the unpredictability of which lethal illness might next wage its attack.

One of the fears I had to face daily was the fear of contact with other people. Everyone was a threat to me because anyone could be carrying the infection that would be my last. That possibility always came to mind when I flew back to the hospital in Houston for treatments. I would sit in my seat and almost shiver, thinking that the stranger sitting next to me might pass along the infectious disease that would kill me. It was ironic to me that there is such a phobia of persons with AIDS. People are so afraid that if an AIDS patient merely breathes on them they will catch the disease. But in reality they are the greater threat. They are the more likely carriers of fatal germs. People fear this strange disease I have, yet their common flu could kill me. But the only antidote to my fear has been trust in God, and I had to focus on the facts that He had brought me as far as I had come and that my life and my death were completely in His hands.

Many strange things happened as I faced the vagaries of my future and my death. Some of those things were hard to understand. One instance occurred in my childhood home in Bryan. After my second bout with pneumonia, my parents took me home with them so I could eat some of my mother's great cooking and regain some strength and weight. It was tough going back home, but I knew I would have to get used to it—my house was up for sale and the appraisers had already valued the furniture that would be sold at auction. I was grateful I had a place to go. I knew it wouldn't be easy on my parents. But with the help of God and some visits to my brothers, I knew we would all get through it.

One night the three of us—Mom, Dad, and myself—stayed up fairly late talking before going to bed. It was one of those rare nights that I was able to sleep. In the middle of a very deep sleep, my mother shook me awake. I was lying on my right side facing the wall, and her voice seemed faint, "Jerry, you have no demons in you, you have no demons in you." At first, when I was still in that half-sleep state, I thought someone had come for me, that perhaps I was being lifted up into heaven. I felt a coolness over all my body as a curtain seemed to be dropping around me. The coolness felt so good. It penetrated every cell in my body. Then I realized that Mother was shaking me.

Mother told me that I was repeating a phrase, "In the name of Jesus, through the power of the Holy Spirit, remove the demons from this body." No one had told me to say that. I had never heard that said before. Mom and Dad said later that I had repeated the phrase nine or ten times before Mom became worried and got up to check on me. As I started to wake from her shaking me, the curtain that had been lowered around me started to go back up, and a sensation of intolerable warmth replaced the coolness. So I kept repeating the phrase Mom told me I had been saying. I kept on repeating it until finally the "curtain" once more lowered around me. I experienced a new peace like I had never felt before.

* * *

I don't understand exactly what happened, but I believe it was then that Satan's powerful grip on my life was loosened. I believe that God drove the sin of homosexuality out of my body. That may not be what happened; I am not *sure*. But I am sure that God is a perfect God and that His hand was right there with me and Mom. She and I witnessed and experienced a miracle of some kind that took place within my body. I was delivered from something very powerful. Once again, as in the emergency room, there was a renewing of my spirit through some miraculous act of God. A healing took place that night. It was a spiritual healing that gave me power and strength to accomplish some things that I wanted to do for the Lord. And I know for sure that on that night there was an emotional healing.

It's difficult to describe what AIDS does to a person mentally and emotionally. Feelings of desolation envelop the mind, and there were times I thought I would lose mine forever. But fortunately I had a Bible and was memorizing some Scriptures that allowed me to stay on track. Philippians 4:7 was one of those that helped me maintain an emotional equilibrium: "And the peace of God, which surpasses all understanding, will guard your hearts and minds through Christ Jesus."

I credit that verse and that night of a strange miracle for being able to stay strong emotionally. Only those who have experienced it can understand how peaceful it can be when the heart and the mind are kept in Christ Jesus. I thank God for the ability to function mentally.

I don't want you to think that just believing in God and quoting Scripture have made all my problems go away. Although I have always come back to normal, there are times when AIDS drives back any feeling of normalcy. Feelings of paranoia are common among AIDS patients. I have often heard patients talk of their fears that friends are being dishonest, that doctors don't really care and are trying to get rich off us. Some patients have written parents out of their wills because they thought their mothers and fathers were poisoning them. And I'm talking about parents who are loving and caring. The AIDS virus works on the mind and causes all those dreadful fears. I've had to face them, too.

In addition to the virus itself, the medication creates its own mental terror. I was one of the first people to take AZT, and its effects were pure torture. AZT is so powerful that in the first few minutes after taking it a rushing sensation splits through the brain. It felt like my head would crack open. Extreme anxiety accompanied each dose. The effect was similar to speed, but with a duller sensation. When I took it I thought that people were talking about me, and my distrust soared. Wherever I was at the time, I didn't want to be there. I couldn't be in a crowd because the drug would cause me to panic. As the drug wore off a bit I returned closer to normal, yet it had to be taken every four hours no matter what.

The problem was that I didn't just stop at normal when the medication's effect wore off. My emotions plummeted past normal into dark chasms of depression and near paralysis. Sensations of grief and hopelessness welled up within me. The swing to the bottom was severe, and I hurt so deeply. But every four hours I reversed directions by taking another dose of AZT and repeating the cycle of mental distress. It never stopped. It continued twenty-four hours every day and night. It was hell on earth. But God sustained me and comforted me. He provided a peace that allowed me to move forward and not give up like so many others were doing.

In April 1987 I once again came down with pneumonia. No one thought I could survive it. I was determined to live through it, however, and once again I made a miraculous recovery. At that point I began to work on this book, and my life became somewhat more secluded. I had little contact with my friends back in Texas, but I called Tony to ask how he was doing and if he was going to church on Sundays. It was so emotional for us to talk and for him to know I was concerned about him. Our conversation ended in tears. For a while I lived with Steve and his wife, Sandy, in Laguna Beach, California. Then I went to stay with Terry, who has four kids and a saint for a wife, Janette. It was beautiful in both locations. What an inspiration to watch the whales in Laguna or the waterfalls and greenery of Tennessee. God's world is so beautiful, and I had never before fully taken the time to notice.

The Bible says God never sends us a problem we cannot handle with His power. It also says He will provide comfort. In both cases, the Scriptures have held true for me. I have grown close to a sweet and loving Jesus and understand that sickness and disease do not come from Him. Our God is there to help us fight the evil forces. I have peace and comfort like I have never felt before, even though I know AIDS continues to ravage my immune system. I pray each night for all who have been afflicted. I pray that God will comfort all of us and all our families. God is a good God and a perfect God.

For me, during these difficult times of struggle, as each day grows darker, a new dawn draws closer. That closeness to the God I love gives me a superhuman peace and sensitivity that keeps me filled with hope for a new and better day.

> Sing, O heavens!
> Be joyful, O earth!
> And break out in singing, O mountains!
> For the LORD has comforted His people,
> And will have mercy on His afflicted.
> —Isaiah 49:13

Part Two

CHAPTER NINE

Some Special Messages to Some Special People

AIDS could end up being the worst epidemic our world has ever experienced. With no cure in sight, it is likely that millions will die from this deadly disease. Right now, as you read this, thousands are dying with AIDS; many of them are alone, with no one willing to care for them. It's a matter of time before everyone knows someone with AIDS.

Worldwide effects are expected to be devastating. In Africa some villages have been almost entirely wiped out because of this epidemic. We in America must take heed, because it is likely that as we glimpse Africa's present, we may well be viewing our future. As the tragedy invades more and more homes, it is becoming obvious that its consequences cannot be ignored. Individuals must determine their response to those caught in the wake of this epidemic. Individuals must choose whether to care for those with the problem or to walk away from them. Whether by giving money to AIDS research or by taking meals to those who are suffering, all of us can play important parts.

To the Church

In the coming years, it will not be possible for the church to ignore the need to minister to the AIDS patient. Few experts think this problem is simply going to go away. People today are dying and need the church to reach out to them. The church must react as Christ would—with love, with acceptance, and without fear. If the church does not respond in a Christian manner, then who will? Who will comfort those who are in such great need? If the church buries its head in the sand, the world will perceive that Christians want to help only when it is convenient or pretty. But if the church leads the way, then the world will perceive that Christians really do care, that God really cares. The church, its members, must set the precedent.

The reaction among the members of my parents' church is an excellent example of a caring response. When I told my parents, at first they were ashamed to tell anyone in the church that I had problems with homosexuality. They did everything they could to prevent anyone from knowing I had AIDS. They were afraid of rejection by the church they had been members of for twenty years. It angered me greatly. It made such a mockery of the church. If my parents could not turn to their church, which they had served so much of their lives, then I felt that it was all a waste. But my parents were wrong about the reaction of that conservative Southern Baptist church in Bryan, Texas.

When I was asked to go on the Trinity Broadcasting Network to talk about AIDS and homosexuality, I knew my appearance would destroy the masquerade that I was dying of leukemia. (I had previously told my parents I didn't want to read any more prayer cards telling me that Mrs. X or Mr. Y was praying for my leukemia. I didn't have leukemia, and I didn't want prayers wasted on a disease that I didn't have.) So I called my parents and told them about the opportunity to tell my story and asked them to pray about whether I should do it. Their response was immediate. They said if it would help just one person, I should do it. The night of the show my parents asked several people from the church to come over and watch a program with them. They told them I would be on it, but they didn't tell them what I would be talking about. When everyone arrived, my father told them the reason that I was going to be on television. Their son had been involved in homosexuality and had been infected with the AIDS virus. They all sat silent and watched the program. Some shed tears; others remained motionless.

When the program ended, one of the finest men in the church, Son Vick, stood up and told the others and my parents what they needed to hear. He said they had all loved me when I was small and they had all loved me when I was in high school. He said they had loved watching me grow and sharing in my successes. He went on to say they would all continue to love me and the rest of the Arterburn family. The other people from the church thanked Mother and Dad for sharing our problem with them and allowing them to help. There was no rejection. There was only love and acceptance from a group of people who really cared. And since that time they have shared their love with me.

The reaction from the pastor of our church was not immediate. I think it took him some time to figure out how he could minister to Mom and Dad and me. But once he did act, he did so in the same manner I believe Christ would have. He brought several of the deacons of the church over to the house one evening. Those staunch men came to me so that I could share communion with them. When we were done, they placed their hands on me and prayed for God to comfort me and to heal me. It was one of the most touching experiences of my life. In my time of greatest need, the church reached out to me. And when my parents needed Christian friends most, they came through for them. We were met with a love beyond anything I or my parents expected. All the negative things I had felt about that church were wiped away with those wonderful acts of caring. My church is the living example of what every church is called to do for the AIDS patient and the family of the AIDS patient.

The church back in Bryan is not the only church that poured out love and ministry to me. When I was in San Antonio, the Reverend Odell Allen and his church were strong in their ministry to me. In fact, I believe their ministry was a direct gift of God. While I was eating one day, Reverend Allen came over to my table and said he believed that God had led him to talk to me and that he sensed that I was very ill. That began a very caring relationship between us. He and his wife would go to any length to show their love. One cold winter's morning, I had nothing in the house to eat and feared going out in the cold. While I was trying to figure out what to do, the doorbell rang. Mrs. Allen was standing at the door with a huge tureen of soup for me. She will never know how good that soup tasted! It represented the care and concern those two Christian people had for me. And they led their whole church in caring that way for me and others in need.

When I was staying in California with Steve, I was able to go to Richard Hogue's church. Through Hal and

Lee Ezell I met Marilyn and Richard, and that's why I was able to do the show on Trinity Broadcasting Network. It would have not been unusual for me to do that program and then receive no further actions of caring, but that didn't happen. Wherever I was, Richard and Marilyn would track me down to call and give some great support and encouragement. On some Sundays they would have Hal stand in for me while the whole congregation prayed. And when I was there, the members would overwhelm me with hugs of love. They were so thoughtful that one could not help but see Christ in them. They and the other churches I have had contact with have helped me beyond measure with their servantlike spirits as they ministered to my needs.

Whatever you feel about homosexuality, you must separate those feelings from AIDS and from those who have the deadly disease. AIDS respects no boundaries, and those who have AIDS are in such great need of ministry.

There are many practical things a church can do to show caring for the AIDS patients. The church can lift the spirits of those sick and hurting people by visiting them. *Visit them in the hospital and in the homes.* Tell them you love them and that God loves them even more. Tell them God cares for them and wants them to be well. Christians are the ones who can best relay that message of hope and strength.

The strength of the AIDS patient lessens as the disease progresses. When someone is known to have the disease, *form a group to help that person with meals or maintenance of the home.* Just going by to visit can lift the person's spirits immeasurably.

The most practical thing the church can do is to *assist the person financially.* Unemployment is the eventual consequence of AIDS. And with income decreased, there is usually an increase in medical bills. Many of those with AIDS are without insurance to pay for the medical help they need. Anything the church can do collectively will go a long way in showing the AIDS patient that God cares.

The church can do no greater service than to *pray for the people who developed AIDS*. This should not replace those practical things that need to be done, but it should not be ignored. The past few months have been the most rewarding that I have lived. I have seen many miracles and have experienced more love than I ever knew existed. I have lived much longer than most who have AIDS, and I believe my endurance is due to the wonderful prayers of the people in churches all over this country. When I receive cards from a group of people who have been praying for me, I know that love alone added another month to my life. Do not discount the role that prayer can have in helping the struggling AIDS patient to feel hope.

I pray that churches in our country and around the world will unite to minister to AIDS patients who so desperately need others to care. I pray that the church will confront irrational fear of this dread disease and fight to comfort those who are afflicted by it. AIDS patients who think they have no hope need the supportive arm of the church to be wrapped around them. They need to be told there is a God who cares. They need someone to explain the hope that can be found in Jesus Christ.

In addition to the AIDS patients, the church needs to address the problem of homosexuality. I realize that to espouse the cause of ministering to the homosexual takes some very special people with a very special calling. It is easier to allow someone else to reach out to that group of people who have been so alienated from the church, but what an important group to help.

Now, because of AIDS, more homosexuals are questioning whether they should get out of that lifestyle. I cannot tell you how many times I have heard some gay person say, "Maybe I should have listened to my Sunday school teacher." There is a movement out of the gay world like I have never seen before.

But even without AIDS, there would still be thousands of homosexuals who want out but have no one to lead the way. These are not bad people. Many are confused people who need your help greatly. Please do not ignore this sector of society. Homosexuals are not members of a distant and remote cult. My first two experiences as a child were with people from the church in church-sponsored functions. These problems probably exist in your church, also.

The hurting homosexual is in hiding. The hurting homosexual needs your help. And nothing can be more rewarding than to help turn someone's life from the emptiness of sin to the wholeness of a relationship with God. Please consider what level of outreach your church has to this group. It is probably nothing. I encourage you to motivate your church leaders to begin a ministry.

To the Family of the AIDS Patient

No people play a greater role in the well-being of the AIDS patient than the family. I am fortunate to have a family that supports me through these dark hours. From the moment I told my mother and father, they both have done nothing but show their extreme love and care for me. They handed me God's love through their own sacrifice to ensure that I was taken care of.

When I needed them the most, they came through for me. They let me know they didn't approve of what I had done, and they accepted it 100 percent when I told them I had repented and turned away from my past. Their forgiveness allowed me to experience an earthly incarnation of Christ's forgiveness for me. My parents have been greatly responsible for the amount of time I have had and the quality of that time.

When I went for treatment at the Institute for Immunological Disorders in Houston, I was exposed to hundreds of AIDS patients who had been abandoned by their families. Not only had some been abandoned, but they had also been literally cast out of their families. They would lie in their rooms for days with no visitors. Their families couldn't cope with the reality of what happens in an imperfect world.

Please don't let your own problems stand in the way of giving to your son or daughter the love and care that he or she needs. Don't spend the rest of your life with the guilt of knowing that when your child needed you the most you didn't help. You may need some professional counseling to help you make it through this difficult experience. Whatever it takes, please, for your sake and the sake of your child, obtain the help you need. If you have already neglected to care for someone in the family, it may not be too late to make amends.

If your child has this disease called AIDS, I beg of you to do what Christ has asked you to do, and that is to love him or her. If you don't, your rejection will intensify the guilt and condemnation that he or she already feels. Please dig deep in your heart and find that love.

To the Parents of a Homosexual Child

I have friends all over this country who have experienced the same battle with homosexuality that I have experienced. These are men and women that any parent would be proud to have as sons or daughters. These men and women need your help and guidance. If you sense that your child is having a problem in the area of sexual preference or identity, I urge you to do possibly the most difficult thing for you to do—discuss it with your child. Bring it out in the open. Once you are able to talk about it, your child will know you will not reject him or her for it. Reject the behavior but not the person; then you will be in a position to help. You might suggest that the entire family seek some counseling together. This alone may cause all of you to reexamine your roles within the family and make some changes. That might motivate your child to make some changes also.

The attraction into the homosexual world is very strong. The rationalizations of why it is okay make it even harder for a person to reject that lifestyle. Leaving the gay life is not something that happens overnight, and there may be many relapses along the way. Please be patient, and don't give up. Your son or daughter may not make it out of the gay lifestyle, but this is no cause for rejection. Continue to show your love and concern. Be sure that your child knows that you are available and willing to help. I know that this is a difficult problem to handle. I watched my parents struggle with it through the years as I struggled also. But through it all, my parents' faith brought them through it. I encourage you to go to your minister and seek his guidance, and don't forget the wisdom of the Scripture. God wants to help you and your child if you will call upon Him to do so.

To the Homosexual

I know you have spent a large portion of your life in a state of confusion. I have been through that and know how painful it is to go without answers. If you are like me, there has always been a little twinge down inside that begs you to question what you are doing. No matter how strong the rationalizations for your lifestyle, you believe it is not what God intended for you. Like me, you probably have come to the realization that if it was right and if everyone were gay, in about eighty years the whole world population would be finished.

Our lifestyle of homosexuality is a counterfeit produced by Satan to keep us from what God wants for us. Satan has gone to a whole bunch of trouble to ensure that we do not experience God's best. Satan would love to kill anyone who wants to serve. He came at me with a double-barreled shotgun, and I can remember the very night he held it to my head and I let it go off. I knew from the very first that what I was involved with was wrong. But it wasn't long until I was able to rationalize the wrong away—and that was when Satan started to rule in my life and prevented me from doing much of what I wanted to accomplish. I hope that you are beyond that by now and are ready to do what is right for yourself and the others around you.

Many of you are being told that there is no way out of homosexuality. You are being convinced that it wasn't your choice to be gay. You have been brainwashed into thinking that you were born homosexual. That belief is everywhere, but it is a lie. It is only justification. It is not the truth. The truth is something that Satan will go to great lengths to prevent you from knowing. When I was younger, I never fully understood just how powerful

Satan is in this world. Now I believe with all my heart that Satan will use any method possible to deceive us. A minister even gave me tapes of sermons where homosexuality is justified and the Bible distorted to do it.

I hope that you can understand that no matter how far into the homosexual lifestyle you have gone, it is never too late to change, it is never too late to go home. God has the power to completely reform you in body, mind, and spirit. Because of what God has done for me, the old Jerry Arterburn has been cut away. He is gone. And I am a new person through the power of God. I believe you want to change. I hope you feel you must change. You have to try. There is a better way. God has a better plan. With the decision to seek God's will for your life, your life can be fulfilling. If you make a decision to leave the homosexual world behind, I want to suggest a plan that could be of help to you.

1. *Get professional help.* The issue of sexual orientation is complex. You need help in sorting it all out and making sense of what has happened. I know of no one who has been able to do this alone and not suffer many painful relapses. There are counselors and psychiatrists who specialize in this and can be of great help. The issue is not whether or not you can do this alone; the issue is why should you attempt it alone when help is available.

2. *Find a church with a caring ministry.* If you have never been to a church you liked, then you need to keep looking. I have talked to many people who don't go to church because they didn't like it when they were young. Churches have changed, and you have changed. The church represents a place where you can find a supportive environment to live the way you want to live. Going to church will also be the first step toward learning what it means to turn your life over to Christ and live

according to His will. Churches are some of the healthiest organizations in existence today, and they want to help you make a new start.

3. *Meditate on the Word of God.* The Bible has become so dear to me since I discovered I had AIDS. I took it for granted for so many years, as many people do who grow up in a church setting. It's easy to regard the Bible as just another book. The worldview is that the Bible is merely a grand piece of ancient literature. But it is not just a book or a collection of literary pieces. It is the very Word of the God who created the universe. In following through with my decision to steer clear of the gay world, the Bible has become incredibly important to me. By utilizing the power and wisdom of God's Word, my life was transformed.

I want to encourage you to get a Bible and begin to memorize some Scriptures. You may want to start with some of the Scriptures that are in this book. Read them. Say them over and over again. Make them a part of your life. Meditate on what they are saying to you. They will allow you to change your entire focus. They will keep you moving toward the goals that God would have you achieve.

4. *Avoid heterosexual relationships for a while.* There is no female or male wonderful enough to solve your problem. Changing your sexual preference is a terrible burden to ask someone else to shoulder. You probably know people who have married, hoping that the opposite sex would heal them of their problem. But relationships with the opposite sex can be too frustrating in the beginning of your new lifestyle. They most likely will lead to failure and cause you to justify a return to the homosexual world saying, "I gave it a try." To become involved too soon is to sabotage your plans to start over.

There will be plenty of time for relationships later. In the beginning it is best to spend some time with new friends while you discover who you really are and who you can become.

5. *Change the places you go and who you go with.* If you are serious about leaving the gay world behind, you must make some sacrifices. You must leave some wonderful friends behind. They cannot be ongoing associates because of the temptations you would face simply by being around them. They could also destroy the confidence you have established. Your desire to change would force them to look at that issue for themselves. Say good-bye to your gay friends and tell them when you are stronger you will once again enjoy their company. That way you will not be rejecting them, yet you will allow yourself to be free from some very powerful influences from the past.

Keep in mind how much Satan wants you to do anything but establish a normal lifestyle. He will go to great lengths to bring you back into a counterfeit culture. He is the master of deception and confusion. If you are to win the battle against Satan, you must utilize every possible resource available.

If I had been more involved with the church and Bible study, I probably would have been better able to handle the temptations of homosexuality. I would not have been so vulnerable. Therein lies the danger for all of us. When we stop growing, we allow Satan to move in and take control or at least to lay the foundation for control. When I was in school I don't think I knew one verse of Scripture by memory. I fed my thoughts and my emotions nothing that would keep me in Christ. I sometimes wonder what would have happened if I had known by heart the following verses. Imagine what I would have been able to withstand if I had committed the following verses to memory:

> Now the body is not for sexual immorality but for the Lord, and the Lord for the body. . . . Do you not know that your bodies are members of Christ? . . . Flee sexual immorality. Every sin that a man does is outside the body, but he who commits sexual immorality sins against his own body. Or do you not know that your body is the temple of the Holy Spirit who is in you, whom you have from God, and you are not your own? For you were bought at a price; therefore glorify God in your body.
>
> —1 Corinthians 6:13–20

Wow! What a piece of Scripture. If I had been grafting that into my mind during those days at A&M, it would have had a great impact on me. God promised that His Word does not return to Him void. It produces results. Young people and older adults must not be deceived into thinking that just being moral or keeping certain behaviors in check is enough to fulfill the Christian life. Satan will use that deception to his advantage and destroy the person who does nothing to grow closer to God. That was certainly how Satan worked on me.

Some other verses that would have been a big help to me if I had committed them to memory are 1 Thessalonians 4:3–6:

> For this is the will of God, your sanctification: that you should abstain from sexual immorality; that each of you should know how to possess his own vessel in sanctification and honor, not in passion of lust, like the Gentiles who do not know God;

that no one should take advantage of and defraud his brother in this matter because *the Lord is the avenger of all such, as we also forewarned you and testified* (emphasis added).

It will not be easy to change your lifestyle, but with the help of God you can do it. I know there seems to be great allure and pleasure, fun and excitement, in the gay lifestyle, but it simply is not worth missing the very core of life itself—service to God. It is never too late to turn to God and ask His help.

To the AIDS Patient

You may believe that AIDS is God's way of taking it out on the homosexual. You may be functioning under the mistaken belief that God does not care anything about you and is in fact punishing you and the rest of the homosexual world for not abiding by His law. It is likely that if you feel that way, you developed it from someone who didn't understand AIDS and didn't understand God. If that was what God was doing, no babies would die of AIDS. If God wanted to punish homosexuals with a disease, He could have developed one that children and hemophiliacs couldn't contract. Don't be misled by some people who speak with the sound of authority but have spent more time speaking than considering the illogic behind the statements. God loves you. Your sins and your problems are no worse than another person's. And God wants to help you in your darkest hour.

God has set up such a perfect, natural world into existence that once any portion of that natural world is violated, whether by adultery or abortion or homosexuality or any other sin, there is going to be a price paid.

The Bible spells it out quite clearly. The Bible does not say that the wages of *God* is death; it says that the wages of *sin* is death (see Romans 6:23). God hasn't caused this to happen to me or to you. Sin has caused it. I regret that I didn't heed this simple warning that I had heard all of my life. I guess I felt so protected, that anything like AIDS couldn't possibly happen to me.

God didn't give you AIDS to force you to worship Him or to pay attention to Him. But now that you have it, you can take the illness as an opportunity to develop a relationship with God. In getting your affairs in order, you can move into the spiritual realm and get things right with a God who loves you and cares greatly about you. I have heard other Christian AIDS patients welcome death. They would rather go on and live with Jesus than remain here and continue to be tempted sexually. They see death as a source of hope, and they are ready for it. I have heard nurses comment on how peaceful death is when one of the patients that dies is a Christian. You can have that peace that transcends all understanding. I hope you will not let some very small people with unloving attitudes keep you away from a very large God who loves you. In Philippians 4:6–7 you can find assurance that as a Christian, you need not worry about anything, and especially not your future.

> Be anxious for nothing, but in everything by prayer and supplication, with thanksgiving, let your requests be made known to God; and the peace of God, which surpasses all understanding, will guard your hearts and minds through Christ Jesus.

I have been so fortunate to experience that peace. That same peace is available to you if you will only ask for it by trusting in Christ Jesus. Believe it or not, this can be a joyous time for you if you will accept Jesus as your Savior. And you can do that right now.

Through all of my trials, I have been able to verify that there is good news in all of this sadness and sorrow. I have found for me and know that for you there is an answer. Jesus Christ is alive today and is healing today. That healing might come in the form of a complete physical healing. Although I know of no one with AIDS who has experienced that kind of complete healing, I know that nothing is impossible for God.

I believe God has given me some extra time to accomplish some things for Him. Since my diagnosis, I have honestly had the best years of my life. Because of Him, they have been filled with meaning and purpose. To do that, He allowed me to experience some physical healing and weight gain while others were deteriorating rapidly around me.

But what is more important than the physical healing is the fact that God will heal you emotionally and spiritually. Through His power you can receive complete restoration of your spirit. Through Christ you may be able to find peace for the first time in your life. You will be able to be at peace with your Creator and with your destiny. In the worst of circumstances, you can find hope and healing and restoration through Jesus Christ. That's the good news.

I have a theory that many AIDS patients are dying before their time because of extreme guilt and condemnation. If you had Jesus Christ in your life and were living with that same spirit that raised Christ from the dead, I believe you would experience life like you never imagined it. You would understand that this is no time to stop living. There are things to be done, and with Christ there is new joy to be found.

In a sense I am grateful for my disease. Before it I never dealt with the reality of life. I skipped through life with an egotistical misunderstanding of what it was all about. The disease has forced me back to the essential truths of life, truths that I found in the teachings and the life of Christ. *I would truly rather live two or three more days with His spirit in me than spend another thirty-six years the way I was living.* The old way just is not worth it. I believe that you know that also. In knowing it, I hope that you, too, will reach out for an eternal hope that is found in Christ.

I want to share the following Scripture with you and encourage you to read it over and over. I believe it is one of the reasons I have lived as long as I have.

> Because he has set his love upon Me,
>   therefore I will deliver him;
> I will set him on high, because he has
>   known My name.
> He shall call upon Me, and I will
>   answer him;
> I will be with him in trouble;
> I will deliver him and honor him.
> With long life I will satisfy him,
> And show him My salvation.
>   —Psalm 91:14–16

I believe that through the hands of a man, God wrote those words years ago so that I could be comforted by those truths today. I know He wants you to know that comfort also. Most people do not realize what a great God we have. I hope you can come to that realization soon. I hope you can experience the comfort God wants to give you. I hope you will become so at peace with yourself and your circumstances that those around you will begin to wonder what is going on with you. I hope you can be transformed and that your mind can be completely renewed. I hope in your struggles you are able to rejoice with me at the opportunity to develop a relationship with our Creator. You can be happy and experience joy because Jesus is alive. He is here for you today.

I pray each day that God's peace and comfort will overcome you. I pray that each of you will know that God loves you. I pray that your parents will be able to respond to you in love. But if they are not strong enough, I pray that you will forgive them. I pray that those parents will have the extra strength that is needed to be joyful even in the times of having a sick child. I pray that your last days will be spent with a joyful family, a united family, a healed family. And I pray that wherever you are, you will be able to claim that you are part of the family of God. If you have been abandoned by your earthly family, I pray that today you will take the first step toward accepting a place with your heavenly family. In their arms you are forever welcome.

CHAPTER TEN

The Hope of Forgiveness

There is a common feeling among those who have AIDS and those who surround the AIDS patient. It is also found among those who struggle to leave the gay world behind. I believe it is found in almost every homosexual that I have met. It is the most devastating and paralyzing of all emotions. I am talking about guilt. Plain, old-fashioned guilt.

Guilt tugs at us and motivates us to take a second look at what we are doing. But if guilt tugs too hard, we try to turn it off or at least lower its intensity. The problem with all our stopgap measures is that they yield only temporary results. When they stop working, our guilt returns with even greater force, thus making even more drastic measures necessary to kill the feeling for a while. The cycle of guilt/relief will continue forever unless a decision is made to stop the behavior that produces the guilt.

Guilt does not lie dormant. It refuses to. It seeps into every fiber of our existence and ladens us with depression and anxiety. It cuts us off from those we want to be close to. We become unable to look people in the eye because of the skeletons that remain in the closets of our past. The ever-active guilt takes its claws and slashes through any sense of well-being we may have. It refuses to go unnoticed. It demands that the bearer pay full attention to its presence. So that we do not forget its power, guilt generates pain that has no physical origin. It saps our energy and leaves us with a fatigue that rest can't satisfy.

Guilt literally makes us sick. Guilty people become ill more than others because our ability to ward off infection is lowered from this negative emotion. For some, the guilt becomes so intense that they begin to hallucinate and see the horrors of life manifested in visions of an unreal world. For others, guilt attacks them through their nightmares, revealing to the subconscious that something is not right and must be attended to. Guilt will not be ignored. The great preacher Charles Spurgeon said, "Beware of no man more than yourself, we carry the worst enemies within us." There is no enemy worse than guilt. It lives within us and destroys our ability to function normally in the world. Where guilt is allowed to prosper, a person will not.

Guilt will not be buried dead. It is always buried alive with a force that few people understand until they become victimized by it. We may try to hide it, but it will not remain hidden very long. We may try to pacify it, but it will not be tamed. Feeding the gnawing, gnashing emotion with food or drugs, sex or work, or any other quick fix will bring only greater frustration and further illness. Guilt cuts us off from others, and such pain-relievers as drinking serve only to intensify our isolation. That isolation also increases our susceptibility to sickness. In Psalm 32 the writer says, "When I kept silent about my sin, my bones wasted away" (v. 3 NASB).

What an accurate description of the effect of a wayward life. A person who contracted AIDS through homosexual activities, and who is struggling to hold onto life as long as possible, could experience nothing more emotionally deadly (or emotionally damaging) than the guilt that comes from knowing he is living with the consequences of a life of sin.

Guilt does more than make us physically sick and cut us off from a long and fruitful life. It causes us to focus only on ourselves. The world of the guilty is the world of the selfish. The person experiencing guilt will not focus on others. Everything revolves around "what I did" or "what I said" or "how I looked." Guilt does not allow for a world of significant others. Guilt forces a self-centeredness that comes from unresolved and unacknowledged sin. The guilty person becomes hypercritical and sees only that which is negative and bad in other people. The guilty person feels everyone else is to blame for whatever goes wrong. And for the chronically guilty person, few others can do things right. Everything becomes a source of disappointment. Life lapses into a joyless subsistence. Eventually, the erstwhile thrill seeker comes full circle to a life that has no contentment.

This hopeless, guilty condition is not experienced only by the homosexual victim of AIDS. Nor is the homosexual the only one to become wrapped in the ugliness of guilt's manifestations. The skeletons in the closets of those involved in heterosexual affairs cause guilt's terror. Divorcees who may not even be responsible for the demise of their marriage experience guilt. Parents know the heavy pain of guilt when they discover that a son or a daughter is addicted to drugs or pregnant out of wedlock or practicing homosexuality.

Guilt is an equal opportunity emotion that knows no bounds in our society. Guilt paralyzes its victims by taking advantage of their ignorance in knowing how to overcome it and their unwillingness to take action to stop its ravages. Guilt can be found wherever people have wandered from God's will.

When someone is found guilty of a crime, that person must pay a price to resolve the harm that has been done. In fact, the word *guilt* actually means "to pay." When we experience guilt, we pay for the crime or sin in our lives. We cannot escape guilt. We may blame God, but in actuality it is our guilt that produces the results that hurt us. In Agatha Christie's mystery novel *The Moving Finger,* one of her characters reveals the force that guilt has on life without God's intervention:

> There's too much tendency to attribute to God the evils that man does of his own free will. God doesn't really need to punish us . . . we're so busy punishing ourselves.

Her theology may not be exactly correct, but the point is well made.

So where is the hope for the person who is trapped by guilt, cut off by remorse, and left hurting by shame? What is the answer for all of us who are found far short of God's will in our lives? Is there only more and more destruction in a spiral of increasingly painful punishment? Fortunately for all of us, God has made a provision that will loosen guilt's grip on our lives and allow us to experience the hope that has escaped us. Hope is available to all of us, no matter what we have done or whom we have harmed.

God knows what He created. He knew that you and I would not be perfect. He knew there was no way for us to live up to His standards; that's why He sent His Son to die for each of us. He knew before any of us were born that we were going to make mistakes, and some big ones at that. God made a big deal out of our forgiveness. If a telegram or a letter would have done, He would have sent one. But that wouldn't have been enough. God's sacrifice is the greatest act of love and compassion in the history of the world. God sent His Son to die for our sins so that we would have everlasting life. Accepting that fact, and allowing Christ to be the Lord of our life, guarantees that we will not have to suffer eternal punishment because of past misdeeds.

We can do other things to resolve the guilt of the past, too. Many Christians trust in Christ but are still plagued by the effects of guilt, even though they know Christ died for their sins. They remain miserable because they don't follow the scriptural principles for forgiveness. God established a three-part plan we can follow. And if we follow His plan, our guilt will be negated and Satan will be rendered impotent to hamper our closer walk with God.

Step one: *Confess your sins to God.* When we trust Christ, our sins are immediately forgiven. But to erase the effects of the sin in our lives, we must continue to make things right with our heavenly Father. Feeling fully forgiven, wiping the slate clean, requires that we take action. We must come before God and admit we have failed—just the opposite of trying to rationalize the sin away or of blaming someone else for our problems. Confession means that we come before God and say that we agree with Him that we have erred and that it is no one's fault but our own. God honors this recognition and open confession of sin, and it allows us to break loose from sin's grip.

The disciple John explained this concept in 1 John 1:9, "If we confess our sins, He is faithful and just to forgive us our sins and to cleanse us from all unrighteousness." That promise has meant so much to me as I have had to face the results of my rebelliousness. Satan would like for me to believe that I am not really forgiven. When some doubt crops up I just quote this Scripture, which is one of my claims to the Christian life today. God's promise does not exclude those who have succumbed to homosexual sin—our sin is no worse than that of the thief or the adulterer. God's promise includes *all* strugglers who have blown it. But confession to God is only the first step in the three-part plan to receive forgiveness.

Step two: *Confess your sins to one another*. A one-dimensional confession is not enough. God intends for us to be involved with one another, and He doesn't intend for us to hide behind shells of secrecy where sin can have a chance to multiply. It is God's plan that we should remain open with other people. We have to be able to say to one another that all is not as it appears, that we have failed, even though we might look successful.

Pride prevents us from wanting to share our problems with others. We don't want a blemish on our "Christian-coated candy shell." Pride only perpetuates sin and its consequences. God wants us to be open to one another. When we are, our sins are forgiven and our guilt fades away. We are healed emotionally. "Confess your trespasses to one another, and pray for one another, that you may be healed" (James 5:16).

We must not fall into the trap of pretension that shuts out the world when we try to be something other than we really are. I remember how accepted I felt when I first entered the world of homosexuality. That acceptance was one of the attractive aspects of gay life. The church must change its ways and openly accept imperfect people by showing God's love and helping them day by day. Other areas of life often appear more open and accepting than the church. In their book *The Edge of Adventure,* Bruce Larson and Keith Miller comment,

> The neighborhood bar is possibly the best counterfeit there is to the fellowship Christ wants to give His church. An accepting, inclusive fellowship. Christ wants His church to be a fellowship where people can come in and say "I'm sunk," "I need help."

If we are to experience God's best for our lives, we must be willing to open up to one another and experience the freedom that comes from confessing our sins to one another. After I discovered I had AIDS, for the first time my brothers and I opened up to one another about our pasts. It felt so good to be able to share with them rather than hide from them. And as Terry and Steve shared with me their past transgressions, I felt the power of forgiveness enter that room with us. There was no condemnation. There was acceptance and the realization that we were each one equal to the other when it came to our capacity for sin. The sins had different labels, but one was no worse than the other.

It was great to dissolve the pretense that separated all of us. If you want to feel the awesome power of forgiveness, you must open up to others and confess your sins and faults to them. Not only will God forgive you, but you will be able to forgive yourself. This is a key step in eliminating the burden of guilt from your life. There is one more step to God's three-part plan to receive forgiveness.

Step three: *Forgive one another*. In the January 9, 1984, issue of *Time*, Lance Morrow, senior editor, wrote a piece entitled "Why Forgive." It was written on the occasion of Pope John Paul II meeting with twenty-six-year-old Turkish terrorist Mehmet Ali Agca to forgive him for an assassination attempt. Morrow wrote:

> Christ preached forgiveness, the loving of one's enemies. It is at the center of the New Testament. Stated nakedly, superficially, the proposition sounds perverse and even self destructive, an invitation to disaster. . . .
>
> Forgiveness is not an impulse that is in much favor. It is a mysterious and sublime idea in many ways. The prevalent style in the world runs more to the high plains drifter, the hard, cold eye of the avenger, to a numb remorselessness. Forgiveness does not look much like a tool for survival in a bad world. But that is what it is.

Nothing can clear a life of excess emotional baggage more than the act of forgiving someone else—unless it would be forgiving yourself.

It is very clear from Scripture that God requires us to forgive others. This is such an important step in the healing of families. A father who discovers he has a homosexual son may be shocked and incredibly disappointed. The anger that might come from that discovery could damage the relationship between the two for a long time or even permanently. The only hope for that son to walk in a normal lifestyle is for the father to patiently help the son find his way back. The son must know his father's love will always be there. The only way this can be possible is for the father to forgive the boy for not being what he had wanted him to become. The father's forgiveness can be the most important element in resolving the conflict within the boy. Moreover, forgiving one another is what God wants us to do. It is His choice of reactions for us to take. In Ephesians 4:32, we are told to forgive one another:

> And be kind to one another, tenderhearted, forgiving one another, even as God in Christ forgave you.

In another Scripture (Matthew 6:14, 15), the forgiveness of one another is revealed as a mandate that must be followed:

> For if you forgive men their trespasses, your heavenly Father will also forgive you. But if you do not forgive men their trespasses, neither will your Father forgive your trespasses.

The reason so many people have not experienced the joy found in God's forgiveness is that they have not forgiven others. Resentment, bitterness, and anger have been allowed to destroy a relationship or many relationships. When that occurs, God does not forgive the person holding the grudge. If you hold a grudge, then you also hold your own condemnation. An unwillingness to allow others to be free of their pasts only keeps us tied to ours. Allowing others to let go of their mistakes frees us from our own in the eyes of God, thereby enabling us to experience the power and freedom of forgiveness. It is time for all of us, especially Christians, who make mistakes daily (and all of us do) to stop hiding. It is time to open up to God and to forgive one another no matter how severe our wrongs. It's time for all of us to walk out of our pasts and into the present.

There is something very special about what God has done. He promised to do the seemingly impossible: forget. God's ability to forget makes Him the perfect God for imperfect people, people unable to live up to all of the standards of the Christian life. God promised that He will not hold past sins against us, "For I will forgive their iniquity, and their sin I will remember no more" (Jeremiah 31:34). God made the same promise in Isaiah 43:25, "I, even I, am He who blots out your transgressions for My own sake; / And I will not remember your sins."

The greatest illustration of God's willingness for us to experience the joy of forgiveness is found in Psalm 103:8–13:

> The LORD is merciful and gracious,
> Slow to anger, and abounding in mercy.
> He will not always strive with us,
> Nor will He keep His anger forever.
> He has not dealt with us according to
>   our sins,
> Nor punished us according to our iniquities.
>
> For as the heavens are high above the
>   earth,
> So great is His mercy toward those who
>   fear Him;
> As far as the east is from the west,
> So far has He removed our
>   transgressions from us.

As a father pities his children,
So the LORD pities those who fear Him.

The verse that says God has taken our sin and removed it as far from us as east is from west is phenomenal. It is significant that the verse does not say as far as north is from south. North appears to be a long way from south at first glance. But if you trace your finger along a globe, moving it further and further north, it eventually tops the north pole and begins moving south. If you move your finger toward south on a globe, then eventually you round the south pole and begin moving north. North and south meet.

Now keep in mind that this passage was written long before Columbus discovered that the world was round. Thousands of years before Columbus, the Scripture refers to the distance God will remove our sins from us as the same distance between east and west. If you trace your finger along a globe going toward the east and you continue around the equator, you find that you never start going west—you continue to move toward the east. East and west never meet. What is the distance between east and west? Infinity. How far does God remove our transgressions and sins from us? As far as infinite space can continue. God wanted us to be sure we knew that once He forgets about a sin it will not be recalled. It is removed from us forever. A lot of people are still feeling guilty about things that God has forgotten long ago. Others are afraid to change because they don't know that God will completely forgive them.

Every person who is alive today is plagued by scars from the past. We live with guilt, shame, and remorse. If we didn't all have those scars, we wouldn't need God, nor would we need anyone else. The human condition is one of imperfection. Rather than living with the fear of being found out, we must allow God to show His redemptive power in our lives. God doesn't want us starting each day with the weight of shame and remorse. He is a specialist at removing our destructive feelings and enabling us to live with love and acceptance.

God alone has the power to move us from victim to victor. He knows all of us will fall short of what He would have us be. He knows we will stumble and fall. But He wants us to know there is no need to wallow in our past failures. God wants us to get up and get on with life. He wants us to learn from our mistakes and share our newfound wisdom with a world desperately in need of answers. God wants us, even though we are tripped up and fallen down, broken and confused. He wants to show us just what He can do with a life that has nothing but heartache and pain as a résumé. Despite our wanting to live with our pasts in self-pity and bitterness, God stands ready to take us in and show us a better way. We cannot afford to let self-pity obscure the hope and forgiveness available. If we do, only Satan benefits from the deception.

There is no need to spend your life trying to compensate for a past that went awry. God wants you to come out of the past. He is counting on your coming out of the past to help others discover the reality of His forgiveness. According to God, your past just ended one second ago.

CHAPTER ELEVEN

The Power of Perseverance

There is no immunity from life's struggles. If you live and breathe, you are going to experience struggle in many forms. For me, I am struggling to survive with AIDS. For my family and friends, they are struggling to help mitigate the ravages of my disease. Others struggle with diseases even more savage than AIDS. Still others struggle with divorces, unfaithful spouses, jobs that fail to deliver promised rewards.

Difficult situations cannot be ignored, yet the temptation is to give up, to quit in the midst of the struggle. But at the worst point of struggle, life can have its greatest meaning for those who persevere and don't give up. Joy can come from digging in and going after life when it would seem easiest to give up.

In my struggle, nothing has been more rewarding than turning to hundreds of passages of Scripture that sound as if they were written just for me in my time of need. For those who have never opened a Bible, a whole library of comfort is waiting to be shared. One of the most comforting of all Scriptures that call us to persevere is found in Hebrews 12. The challenge is inspiring, and the example of Christ reveals that He has experienced the hurt and alienation that I and others with AIDS have experienced. Whatever pain in whatever form, Christ has experienced it and understands the suffering that comes from it.

> Therefore we also, since we are surrounded by so great a cloud of witnesses, let us lay aside every weight, and the sin which so easily ensnares us, and let us run with endurance the race that is set before us, looking unto Jesus, the author and finisher of our faith, who for the joy that was set before Him endured the cross, despising the shame, and has sat down at the right hand of the throne of God. For consider Him who endured such hostility from sinners against Himself, lest you become weary and discouraged in your souls. . . . Therefore strengthen the hands which hang down, and the feeble knees, and make straight paths for your feet, so that what is lame may not be dislocated, but rather be healed.
> —Hebrews 12:1–3, 12–13

Running the race with endurance. At the point of greatest pain and heartache, that must remain the goal. We mustn't lose hope and give up. We must continue no matter what has befallen us. No matter how wonderful things were before, and how terrible they may appear now, we must run the race marked out for each one of us. An Olympic runner was asked how he faced each race mentally to ensure the greatest possibility of winning. He said he didn't think about past victories, nor past defeats. He thought only about the finish line.

We must press on when the temptation to quit is at its greatest. Our future before us is today, and we can make of it what we want. We can take the time to be what we want. To do anything less is a form of suicide. The challenge is to press on, and in pressing on, to create beauty around us in whatever form we can.

The famous French painters Matisse and Renoir were friends and shared some meaningful times together. Renoir developed a progressively painful case of arthritis and was almost paralyzed by it. But as difficult and painful as it was, he continued to paint. Each brush stroke hurt him severely. One day his friend Matisse was watching him wince as his strokes almost made him double over from the pain. Matisse was moved by Renoir's desperate effort to create at great personal sacrifice. He asked Renoir why he continued under such distress. Renoir replied, "Because the beauty remains: the pain passes." What a powerful message for those of us who are painfully struggling to create something from our lives. We must continue.

I am fortunate to have an illness that has given me time to contribute. Others are cut off from life instantly without the opportunity to refocus and create value from their experiences. Each day grows more difficult for me, but each day I can put something back into the lives of those who care about me and even those who do not. If you are experiencing an illness that is causing you pain and distress, don't give up. You can always give up another day. Persevere. And in persevering, find the areas where you can leave some beauty once the pain subsides. What you are facing may be the worst circumstances of your life, and to make the circumstances even worse, you may feel totally helpless to do anything to change them. You may feel that your days are without hope because you are unable to find any meaning in your struggles. I have had many days like that. But once again, the Bible shows where meaning and purpose can be found:

> Consider it pure joy, my brothers, whenever you face trials of many kinds, because you know that the testing of your faith develops perseverance. Perseverance must finish its work so that you may be mature and complete, not lacking anything.
> —James 1:2–4 NIV

When I read those words, I think back to the time before I became ill. I had the ability to live my life as I chose. And with all those choices before me, I nevertheless missed life altogether. It took AIDS to set life before me in a way I could finally understand. I missed reality until the realities of limited time and tremendous struggle presented themselves. Only then did I focus on those things that are meaningful and have purpose. Only then did I cease caring about the mundane. I began to look at those things that were life at its best—caring about others more than myself, giving, loving, sharing, and sacrificing. Those are the things that wisdom is made of. I missed them for most of my life until my personal trials forced me to focus on them.

> Blessed is the man who perseveres under trial, because when he has stood the test, he will receive the crown of life that God has promised to those who love him.
> —James 1:12 NIV

That crown of life is available to all of us, no matter how far we have come and no matter how often we have failed. We are blessed if in the midst of our darkest struggle we persevere or endure to the end. How ironic it is that we often must be faced with death before we can understand life. How fantastic it is to receive the promises of God through endurance: "For you have need of endurance, so that after you have done the will of God, you may receive the promise (Hebrews 10:36).

It is much easier to talk of endurance than to do it, because it requires courage. Being courageous is being equal to the problems and the challenges that are ahead. It is the art of achievement in the midst of fear. If there were no fear, there would be no need for courage. The courageous are filled with many fears, and yet they do not succumb. The courageous defeat fear as they act in the face of its terror. Any fear can be overcome. We must reach out to others who have experienced that same fear, allowing them to continue to conquer their fear by helping us with ours. At times, that can be the most courageous act of all.

Another element besides courage is essential in order to persevere. That element is faith. If we allow our faith in God to rule our hearts, fear can do little to deter us. When we come to the end of ourself, faith will take us the extra distance. I have no idea how those without faith survive. I believe they die before their time, having missed the opportunity to fulfill their potential. For me, when there is nothing else left, there remains faith. Faith helps me continue one more day in my efforts to take my tragedy and bring joy from it to others.

The faith we have in God is important if we are to have faith in ourselves. A story from the golfing world illustrates this point. Patty Sheahan, from Middlebury, Vermont, grew up with three brothers. Her dad was a coach, and so she learned very young to compete. Early in life she took up golf and found that she was very good. In 1983 she competed in the LPGA Championship. She didn't play all that well and wound up seven strokes behind the leader. Her manager decided that for Patty it was over. She couldn't see any way that Patty could win. The manager told Patty she wanted to take an early flight out, but Patty told her not to do it. She said she had decided to win the game. As Patty persevered through the next holes, she birdied the five that followed and won the entire tournament. The clear message to all of us who suffer from a terminal illness is this: *You never want to be on an early flight out, just before the victory is about to be won.* Too many people give up too soon; don't be one of them. Persevere to the end and receive the prize, the reward of a life lived with wisdom and understanding.

I want to challenge you to wipe from your existence any wait-and-see attitude you might have. People who wait and see do not persevere toward the prize. If something is missing from your life, you cannot simply sit around to wait and see if it will show up. If something is missing, you must go after it and work to achieve it. If you cannot name one meaningful thing you have done for someone else, then it's time you take whatever strength you have and do something. A phone call or a letter can be enough to provide hope to someone who might not have had it without your encouragement. It is up to you. When you decide to persevere, you become one who thinks in terms of "I can" and "I will." There is no "I'll wait and see."

It's easy to become distracted from your purpose or to be so depressed you don't feel you can go on. But it is incredible what can be accomplished once you decide you're going to do the best you can with what you have. You may feel inferior to others and may think that your contribution will only be minimal. But you can do great things with the will to do them. Calvin Coolidge put into perspective how much can be done from the willing spirit:

> Nothing in this world can take the place of persistence. Talent will not; nothing is more common than unsuccessful men with talent. Genius will not; unrewarded genius is almost a proverb. Education will not; the world is full of educated derelicts. Persistence and determination alone are omnipotent. The slogan "press on" has solved and always will solve the problems of the human race.

Of course not all of the problems of the human race can be solved with the "press on" attitude, but none of your own can be solved without it. The achievements of the rich, the educated, and the talented are not to be compared with what you can accomplish from your circumstances if you decide to do it. You must be the one to leave self-pity behind and to move into gear. Only you can determine what to do and when to do it. The determination you muster will create its own value in the world. Others will see your persevering spirit and will be motivated by it. They will go beyond what they thought were their limitations because they have seen you make the decision to press on.

The big problem comes when we focus on our limitations rather than our opportunities, when we live with reference to our restrictions rather than awareness of our potential. When we stop limiting ourselves, we do the remarkable. When we take what we have and do with it the best we can, we discover just how much we can accomplish. Here is how Gerald W. Paul said it·

Our lives are somewhat fixed by fate, partly in the cards. The power of positive thinking will not turn paraplegics into quarterbacks or the blind into astronomers.

But while a leopard can't change its spots, it can change its habits. Genes may make us susceptible to diabetes, but we can reduce risk by avoiding obesity. Nature may play a role in lung cancer, but we can quit smoking. . . . For in life, as in poker, you don't need a royal flush to be a winner. Sometimes a pair of deuces—a weak hand played well—is plenty.

You may feel like your hand is pretty weak right now, but you can still play it well. The spirit that perseveres stays in the game. To quit because your cards aren't the best is to miss the great challenge. Winning without an opponent produces no satisfaction, but winning when holding a poor hand produces the greatest rewards imaginable. I don't know what your pair of deuces are, but I am sure God will help you play them well.

It is inspiring for me to read what others have said about perseverance. It helps me know that others understand the challenge I am facing, that others have put into words how that challenge can bring rewards. The great writer Zane Grey said it this way:

To bear up under loss, to fight the bitterness of defeat and the weakness of grief, to be victor over anger, to smile when tears are close, to resist evil men and base instincts, to hate, hate and to love, love, to go on when it would seem good to die, to seek ever after the glory and the dream, to look up with unquenchable faith in something evermore about to be, that is what any man can do, and so be great.

I hope you will decide to be the victor over your circumstances, your illness, and your past. Here is how Theodore Roosevelt put it:

> The credit belongs to the man who is actually in the arena; whose face is marred by dust and sweat and blood; who strives valiantly; who errs and comes short again and again; who knows the great enthusiasms, the great devotions, and spends himself in a worthy cause; who at the best knows in the end the triumph of high achievement; and who, at the worst, if he fails, at least fails while daring greatly, so that his place shall never be with those cold and timid souls who know neither victory nor defeat.

The mere act of persevering after defeat is in itself victory enough. I would imagine that you are like me in that you can list many things that would be classified as failures. But at least we are in the arena trying to accomplish things while others are on the sidelines or in the stands, uninvolved. Look back and be glad you are a participant in this world. Then take that same spirit and move forward each day and face the challenges with a sense of destiny. Make your mark on this world by affecting those close to you with your will to live and your desire to persevere.

One final quote puts our struggles in perspective:

> Therefore, having been justified by faith, we have peace with God through our Lord Jesus Christ, through whom also we have access by faith into

this grace in which we stand, and rejoice in hope of the glory of God. And not only that, but we also glory in tribulations, knowing that tribulation produces perseverance; and perseverance, character; and character, hope. Now hope does not disappoint us, because the love of God has been poured out in our hearts by the Holy Spirit who was given to us.

—Romans 5:1–5

The very act of suffering produces the ability to persevere. When we feel like we have reached our limit, we discover that we can go further because our ability to endure has been enhanced. By the same process, we also grow in character. Suffering tends to eliminate that which is mere waste and froth. Our character can be developed by the very adversity that threatens our life. That is what is so great about God—He can work wondrous results from the most disastrous circumstances. And He promises that when we allow Him to do His perfect work in us, the character we develop will allow us to grow beyond the immaturity of self-centered existence.

If you feel hopeless, there is something you can do about it today. You can make the life-changing decision to persevere with the help and the hope of God. You alone can make that decision. Once you do, you will find deep peace. I challenge you to make the decision to persevere, persevere even if someone has told you that you will not make it through the next night. You just keep on persevering. I believe you will find that it is not the illness or the medication or the circumstances you are up against. I believe you will find that the only thing you are up against is your own attitude. The good news is that an attitude can be changed in an instant. You can change yours right now by changing what you think and what you believe. Life is never so difficult that you are helpless, and an attitude of perseverance can be your ultimate tool for success.

All of us at some time have been knocked down and dragged through the dirt and gravel and have been left cut and bruised. The temptation is to stay down and call attention to our miserable condition. Anyone can get knocked down and stay down. It doesn't take courage to wallow in those ashes of defeat. When discouraged, anyone can give up. It doesn't take a special person to quit. But those who persevere, those who hold onto faith, allow the hard knocks of life to hammer them into valuable vessels containing the character of Christ. Perseverance isn't easy, but its alternative is further defeat and stagnation. The Christian life calls for something better. The reward is not for perfection, but for perseverance. The one who perseveres claims the eternal prize.

As I finish the writing of this book, I continue with the hope of God and a strong determination to persevere. Only God knows my future here on earth. I do not concern myself with how many days or months or years are in His plan. I only know I would rather live one day as I am today than for eternity the way I was.

God bless you as you continue to persevere and search for truth. I hope your search will lead you to my Savior and that we will spend eternity in a better place together.

That State of Love

As the tides of the sea bare down on me
And the sea gulls fly around about me
There on the beach I long to be
To engulf myself in the Heavens.

And wind that whistles thru the reeds
And sand that blows 'cross the sunset
Take my heart to ecstasy
As recalling childhood dreams.

And, oh, the harbor with its sailboats so lonely
And birds encircling round about them
Oh, I would paint a picture of pinks and blues
And hang it in the halls of heaven.

Oh, Lord, the sky is crystalline blue
And the air is refreshingly clean
So restore my mind to that state of love
Where life and all friendships cling.

Jerry Arterburn
1950–1988

Postscript

On June 13, 1988, my son Jerry died peacefully in his sleep. It was the end of his struggle. It was also the end of the most difficult three days in my life, days when I knew Jerry's final hours were upon him. I felt helpless. I tried hard to make him as comfortable as possible, futilely trying to keep his mouth and throat clear of liquid as I fed him, an impossible task.

The weaker Jerry's physical condition, however, the stronger his godly wisdom. Colossians 3:12–14 ("Therefore, as the elect of God . . . put on love, which is the bond of perfection") came to be his favorite Scripture.

Jerry was the number-two son, a good baby, and a delight to care for. As he grew older, his achievements were above average. I was proud when his model of a house, complete with landscaping, won the state competition. Each succeeding accomplishment—culminating with the grand opening of Dominion Housing Development—brought me even more joy and pride in my son. Jerry made it a point to include Clara and me in his celebrations.

But just as Jerry brought me many of the great moments in my life, he also brought some difficult ones. I was crushed and devastated when I found out that Jerry was into the gay lifestyle. When I learned he had AIDS, I was deeply grieved. I questioned God's will. I finally rested, however, when I realized I had to leave everything to God. Spiritually, I placed Jerry in His hands. From that moment we dared not look ahead at a future we could not control, and we refused to look back at a past we could not change.

Clara and I loved Jerry and wanted to care for him. Although we feared rejection from our friends—especially when we consented to his appearance on national television—we knew we couldn't reject him when he needed us the most. Our home would always be open to Jerry.

Terry, his older brother, opened his home in Tennessee to Jerry for several months. His wife, Janette, and their four children, Chris, Yancey, Nikki, and Marcie, loved Jerry dearly and spent many hours waiting on him, praying with him, and giving him the support he badly needed.

Steve, our youngest son, and his wife, Sandy, also opened their home in California to Jerry. One of our most fulfilling moments came last year when Clara and I found a note Jerry had written before leaving for a while to stay with Steve and Sandy:

> Mom and Dad, there would be no way of my understanding your pain or your fear. Like me, you are wondering how we are going to make it through another day. I hope you use this time while I am away to relax and renew your bodies

and minds. You two have been wonderful parents. What we're going through would be a challenge for the saintliest. God's plan for all our lives will soon be revealed. And then onto our reward in heaven. Praise His Holy Name, Jesus.

Love, Jerry

When Jerry was in Bryan, Clara read the Bible to him every night and sometimes in between. She was always there, even though each new complication of his illness magnified her hurt. I love her for who she is and for who she became through that challenge. Her attitudes and actions were those of a godly woman and a Christian mother.

Special moments with Jerry gave us all memories we will cherish. I had built a bird feeder outside his window so he could watch the birds as they fed. One evening when Terry and Steve had flown in, we were all in Jerry's room watching an unexpected guest, a squirrel, come down the tree and help himself from the feeder. Steve was on the bed with Jerry; Terry and Clara were in chairs beside the bed, and I was leaning in the doorway. Clara asked Jerry if she could get him anything. He replied so warmly, "I have all I want. I have my family and God with me. That's all I need."

Another night, when we were all in the den, the boys laughed and cut up with each other as Jerry planned his funeral service down to the last song. Jerry told us, "The only thing I regret is that I won't be around to enjoy the service with you."

The Saturday before Jerry died, I read the twenty-first chapter of Revelation to him. The picture of heaven was real to both of us, and I knew he was ready for what lay ahead.

Jerry's funeral was June 15, 1988, at the First Baptist Church in Bryan. Everyone whom Jerry had asked to have a part in the service had accepted. It was a very special time. We were surrounded by members of the church whose support had enabled us to endure the challenges we faced.

The service was truly worshipful and lessened our grief. The words gave glory to the Lord, and the music offered praise to God. The theme of the service was Romans 8:28, "And we know that all things work together for good to those who love God, to those who are the called according to His purpose."

Our pastor proclaimed that because of Jerry's courage in telling his story, thousands of lives are being changed. At the conclusion of the service, Jerry's casket was rolled down the aisle while we sang, "When We All Get to Heaven." That is when I said good-bye to Jerry, knowing that we would meet again face to face.

Jerry's death was a victory in the face of defeat. Shortly before he died, Jerry said to me, "I have fought a battle with Satan, and God has won the victory."

A thankful father,

Walter Arterburn
July 13, 1988

Resources

For general information on AIDS:

Telephone   U.S. Public Health Service Hotline
1-800-342-AIDS

or

Write   AIDS
P.O. Box 14252
Washington, DC 20044

For Christian counseling resources about homosexuality and AIDS, contact the coalition of ex-gay ministries for the nearest ministry in the United States, South Pacific, or Europe:

Telephone   1-415-454-1017

or

Write   Exodus International
P.O. Box 2121
San Rafael, CA 94912

For locations of live-in AIDS facilities or hospice settings:

Telephone 1-305-463-0848
or
Write Worthy Creations Ministry
3601 Davie Boulevard
Fort Lauderdale, FL 33312

For church education programs and other AIDS-related services:

Telephone 1-213-395-9137
or
Write Desert Stream Ministries
c/o A.R.M. (AIDS Resource
Ministries)
1415 Santa Monica Mall, Suite 201
Santa Monica, CA 90401

Jerry's story, as told by him on videotape or audiocassette, is available. It is especially valuable for young people who are making life and death decisions about sex every day. It is an excellent resource for discussing the issues of homosexuality and AIDS from a Christian perspective.

For a copy of this moving videotape or audiocassette, write to:

Outreach Ministries
Tape Offers
905 Canyon View
Laguna Beach, California 92651

or telephone
714-494-8894

Videotape $22, audiotape $10, including postage & handling.